Take a Knee

**Humorous and Inspiring
Devotionals from
the World of Sports**

by Steve Davis

VA

Vabella Publishing
P.O. Box 1052

Carrollton, Georgia 30112
www.vabella.com

Cover design by Susan Mashburn

Cover photograph "Team Prayer" by Bill Andrews

Manufactured in the United States of America

13-digit ISBN 978-0-9712204-4-7

Library of Congress Control Number: 2008932740

11 10 9 8 7 6 5 4 3 2

Contents

Chapter One
Baseball

Chapter Two
Basketball

Chapter Three
Football

Chapter Four
Golf

Chapter Five

Catchall

(Wrestling, Bobsledding, Bicycling, Camping, ESPN, Boxing, Soccer, Horse Racing, Hockey)

Introduction

In 1992, Gatorade ran a series of ads about the legendary basketball player and icon, Michael Jordan. The series was called "Be like Mike." I tried. I went to the backyard with my basketball and tried the "alley oop" but there was more alley than oop. I tried his 360° windmill dunk, but did more like a 10° lay-up. I tried his long-range threes and came up with short-range twos. As hard as I tried, I couldn't be like Mike.

Which brings me to my older brother, Mike. He introduced me to sports, which he loved dearly. Because of his recent death, I am dedicating the book to his memory. And I am also going to try to "be like Mike" in the way that he nurtured his friendships. People are lucky if they have one or two really good friends. Mike had several. Some had been friends for fifty years. One of his friends said at his funeral, "Mike was the most loyal friend I ever had." I'm going to nurture my friendships in memory of my brother.

All of these stories in this book have appeared in my church's newsletter over the years and as such, are a reflection of what was happening in my life at a particular point in time. They also reflect the sports that either I or our son, Tyler, (please forgive the constant references to him, my wife, Sheri and our little girl, Natalie) have played or loved. With that in mind, if you love tennis or gymnastics, then accept my apologies. Those sports, and some others, are not in the book.

I trust that this book will be helpful to moms and dads, coaches and to the many kids and adults, like me, who love to play the game.

A special thanks goes out to my secretarial staff at the church, including Tara Hafer, Pat Grimes and especially Susan Mashburn. To those who helped edit, Dr. Sonja Bagby, Brian Edwards, Jennifer Jindrich, Larry Insko, and Dr. Eric Holleyman, thanks. Also, the book would not have been possible without my friend John Bell, who has his own impressive career as a writer of sports books and whose help has been invaluable to me.

To Mike

Chapter One

Baseball

Fuddy-duddies

It happens every winter, so I should be used to it. But I am not. I don't understand how it can happen every single year. This year ('07) it happened to Cal Ripken Jr., and so I am really riled up. What happens every year and happened this year to Cal is that someone or several someones, voted against Cal Ripken Jr. for admission to the Baseball Hall of Fame. Oh he got in,

---

I don't get a vote on the Baseball Hall of Fame, but I do get to cast my ballot on how I will live my life.

---

but my point is that there has never been a unanimous selection to Cooperstown. Can you believe that? Was Babe Ruth unanimous? Nope. Ty Cobb? Nope. Hank Aaron? Nope. In fact, Cal Ripken Jr. did finish with the third highest total ever, behind Tom Seaver and Nolan Ryan, but he wasn't unanimous.

How could anyone in their right mind not vote for Cal? Maybe the question contains the answer. They aren't in their right mind. Apparently, some sports writers, living in a home for fuddy-duddies, have decided that nothing should be unanimous, and so they vote against everything. If they had a vote on sainthood, they would cast it against Mother Teresa. They are the Simon

Cowells ("American Idol" judge) of the sports world. The dictionary defines a fuddy-duddy as "One who is old fashioned and fussy."

It is easier to find fault than it is to shower praise. I don't want to be "fussy" and oppose every good idea that comes my way. I want to be positive rather than negative. I want to give a "thumb's up," not a "thumb's down." I don't have a vote for the Baseball Hall of Fame, but I do get to cast my ballot on how I will live my life. As a Christian, I will try to lift people up and not tear them down. I will try to be a positive influence on my team and on the church. I will vote against fuddy-duddyism. Will you join me? Let's make it unanimous!

For Reflection and Discussion

• How will being positive make more of a difference on your team than being negative?
• How can you encourage the negative forces on your team to be positive?
• How do you remain upbeat when things aren't going well?

Scripture: "But encourage one another day after day..." (Hebrews 3:13).

Prayer: "Lord, enable me to remain positive even when things aren't going well for me personally or for the team. And help me to encourage my teammates and coaches and always be a good influence on the team. Amen."

Baseball

Call Me "Coach"

Baseball season is here, and "yours truly" is assistant coach for our son's team, which consists of 8-year olds. Emphasis on *assistant*. I'm trying to act like a coach. I say things that coaches say, like, "Atta boy!" and "Wait for a good one." Apparently I am not succeeding at looking like a coach, at least not to our son. On at least two occasions he has said, "Dad, if you're going to coach, you need some cleats." Translation: my son is embarrassed that his dad wears running shoes and not baseball cleats to the games.

A minister friend of mine who has his doctorate in theology was asked by his then 5-year-old daughter, "Dad, are you a doctor, 'cause some people call you doctor?" "Yes," he replied, "I reckon you could say that." "But Daddy, you can't be a doctor," she blurted out. "Oh? Why not?" he asked. "'Cause you don't even have a kit!" (Doctors, in the old days, used to carry kits.) That begs the question of what is in a doctor's kit. I suppose it would have in it things like a stethoscope, thermometer, and lots and lots of medicine. It would also, hopefully, have a good "bedside manner."

Sure, real doctors have kits and real coaches have cleats. I'm neither, but I'm going to be the best coach I can be – cleat-less. So, what makes a coach, besides cleats?

Can humility be reconciled with greatness? Does humility conflict with confidence?

Great coaches need knowledge of the game, experience in the game, skill in handling players, sound strategy, and the ability to inspire. Coaching is hard, and I

4

understand that many coaches feel inadequate to the task.

That's like ministers. I think of the many times that I have entered a hospital room or funeral home and didn't know what to say or do. I know. I know. I've been to seminary, just like the doctor has been to medical school, but it didn't prepare me for every situation. And dressing like a minister, complete with matching tie and hanky, no more makes me one than wearing cleats makes me a coach.

So, whether we are a coach, doctor, minister or ditch digger, we should all approach our calling with the greatest of humility. We don't know it all, and we approach each day, each game, each Sunday with a dependence upon the Lord to help us do our best.

For Reflection and Discussion

• Can humility be reconciled with greatness? Does humility conflict with confidence?
• How do we overcome our feelings of inadequacy in our chosen vocation?

Scripture: "God is opposed to the proud, but gives grace to the humble" (James 4:6).

Prayer: "Lord, our maker, remind us of our inadequacies so that we might in turn, depend upon you. Give us confidence to do our work, along with a healthy dose of humility. Amen."

E-5

When our son was five, I started calling him "buddy," as in "Hey, buddy, what's happening?" One day he said, "Dad, don't call me 'buddy' anymore." "OK," I said. "What do you want me to call you?" "Chipper," he said. (Chipper Jones is the third baseman for the Atlanta Braves.)

I'm sure Chipper Jones realizes by now that he is idolized by thousands of kids like Tyler. Much discussion has gone on in public circles about whether athletes are role models. Charles Barkley has argued that professional athletes should not be viewed as such, but that parents should be. Of course, like it or not, athletes are idolized by kids, and many kids don't have good parents.

Chipper hasn't asked to be a hero to my son. All Chipper wanted to be, I guess, was a ballplayer. But he is now thrust into the role of icon to 5-year olds. He

---

But wouldn't it be great if a child's heroes were his mom and dad?

---

seems like a really nice man and a heck of a ballplayer. I hope he is a good guy. A lot of little kids are watching. When a third baseman in baseball makes an error, it is scored officially as an "E-5." Chipper is not perfect on the field or off. He will err in both places. You don't have to be perfect, however, to be a good role model.

I'm trying to teach my son that ballplayers are just people – error prone. But Tyler needs some heroes. I suggested to him that school teachers are some of life's greatest role models. And ministers? I can only hope. Social workers? Coaches? Doctors? All yes. But, wouldn't it be great if a child's heroes were his mom and dad?

For Reflection and Discussion

• How can we get kids to focus more on the role models closer to home instead of those on the TV and movie screen?
• Since none of us are perfect, how do we remain good examples for kids, in spite of our flaws?

Scripture: "...show yourself an example of those who believe" (1 Timothy 4:12).

Prayer: "Lord, help me to be honest about my own shortcomings, but also remind me daily that others are watching me. Enable me to set a good example in speech and conduct as one who professes faith in Christ. Amen"

Baseball Fever

"Baseball fever" is a phrase generally used to describe how someone who loves baseball feels about the game, as in, "I love baseball so much I've got baseball fever." Well, I've got a new meaning for it. A few years ago, we signed our son up to play in two leagues at the same time during the summer. Big mistake. Guess what? The two seasons overlapped. One week we had several games on Friday and Saturday, with practices on every other day, except Sunday. (This is the scheduling dilemma that modern parents face when their kids love sports.)

But games and practices aren't ever enough at the Davis' household. No. We eat and sleep baseball. We practice in the backyard. In the house, the couch cushions become bases. I'm the pitcher. Sheri, my wife, is the ump (typecasting). The Atlanta Braves starting lineup is posted in our living room.

Well, I've had enough. I've got baseball fever, 102 degrees Fahrenheit. I'm sick of it. I may take two

---

Any good thing, including preaching and sports, in excess, can be bad.

---

aspirin and go to bed till this season is over. Whatever happened to moderation? Another word for moderation is temperance. For example, a person who is "quick to anger" is called intemperate. Temperance even extends to moderation in physical exercise and sports.

Any good thing, including sports (and preaching), in excess can be bad. Food is one example. We call it gluttony. Work is another. Some people don't know how to pull back and rest. Work becomes their god. By the way, there's a commandment (the fourth of ten) to deal with that one: "Remember the Sabbath day, to keep it holy."

I love the "Wizard of Id" comic strip where the preacher is preaching on moderation. He exclaims: "Moderation is the key to living...eat moderation, drink moderation, work moderation, play moderation, live moderation." After the service, someone passed by, shook hands with the preacher and said: "I think you overdid it."

For Reflection and Discussion

• How important is self-control in your life?
• How do we learn to make commitments and forego immediate gratification?
• What do we do when our culture pushes us to go nonstop and our faith tells us to slow down?

Scripture: "But the fruit of the Spirit is...temperance" (Galatians 5:22-23).

Prayer: "Almighty God, it is a struggle in my soul to live life in moderation. I know that too much of any thing, even a good thing, is bad. I need your Spirit living in me to enable me to choose what is good, to set priorities and to keep them. Amen."

"Holy Cow"

When I was a teenager, I was interested in three things: sports, sports and sports. Girls were way down the list. Baseball was big to me. Professional baseball had an unusually strong appeal – the St. Louis Cardinals, in particular. The Atlanta Braves, our local team, was so bad in those years that I couldn't bear to follow them.

I got interested in the Cardinals and started listening to their games on KMOX radio out of St. Louis. I got hooked. The Cardinals had such stars as Lou Brock and Bob Gibson, but the real star was Harry Caray, who, along with Jack Buck, did the radio broadcast. They were phenomenal. The game came alive over the radio. I listened every night. While other teenagers were in

---

Christians should be full of enthusiasm about their faith and want to share it.

---

their cars with their dates at the drive-in, I was in my car with Harry Caray. Sometimes the radio reception wasn't so great, but it mattered not. Static couldn't hold Harry down. To hear Harry call a home run was like being there: "There's a drive, it could be, it may be, *holy cow*, it is, a home run!!"

Since those years, I naturally followed his career with the White Sox and the Cubs. Through the cable TV station in Chicago, Harry became a national treasure. His seventh inning stretch rendition of "Take Me Out to the Ballgame" was the stuff of legends. To true Harry fans, it didn't matter that he often got the ball and strike count wrong or that he occasionally didn't seem to know who the Cubs were playing. For Harry Caray, the details didn't seem to matter. What mattered was his unabashed enthusiasm for the game. He loved the game. Steve Stone, Caray's partner in the Cubs' booth said: "He is the best salesman of the game..." I was saddened to hear of Harry's death a few years ago, but happy that up to the end, he never lost his enthusiasm.

The word enthusiasm is Greek, *en theos*, or "in God." Christians should be full of enthusiasm about their faith and want to share it. We each have a microphone and a message. Let's take it out to the highways and hedges (or the Wrigley Field ivy) and invite others to a front row seat.

For Reflection and Discussion

• How important is it that we not only live out our faith but be willing to talk about it was well?
• Don't we all go through dry spells in our faith? When we do, how do we come out of it and regain our enthusiasm?

Scripture: "And from that city many of the Samaritans believed in Him because of the word of the woman who testified..." (John 4:39).

Prayer: "Father, sometimes I am excited to be a Christian but lack the courage to tell others. Give me strength. At other times, my enthusiasm wanes and I need reassurance of your presence. Either way, may my life be more consistent as a witness for you. Amen."

"I Shouldn't Have..."

Being a first-base coach for a boys (7/8-year-old) baseball team is not too difficult. You have to tell a kid whether to stay on first or go on to second should their hit get through the infield. In a recent game, I brought shame to all the first-base coaches in the world. We all make mistakes, but when I do, it's always a whopper.

Our son Tyler was at the plate and hit a grounder to the pitcher. As he hustled down the line, the pitcher threw to the first baseman. It looked like a sure out. Well, nothing is sure in this league. The first baseman dropped the ball. Said ball rolled about a foot away – two or three feet, tops. Something compelled me

---

When we accept our own limitations, we become candidates for grace.

(temporary insanity) to say to my son as he crossed first base: "Go to second." I should have said, "Stay on first." I should have. I should have. I should have. I didn't. Well, he obeyed his coach and headed for second. The first baseman threw to second and Tyler was out by a country mile.

If Tyler has said to me once, he has said to me fifty times since then: "You shouldn't have sent me." His first words Sunday morning, after I woke him up with "Good morning, son" were "You shouldn't have sent me." Sheri, my wife said it to me. Our dog said it to me. The neighbors. Total strangers. How about a billboard with "You shouldn't have sent him" and a picture of me in prison garb? Two days later: "Good night son, I love you." "Good night, dad. But, you shouldn't have sent me to second."

Okay. Okay, I get the point. After I crawl out from under this dugout, I'm going to try to forgive myself for my, oh, so public, *faux pas*. Our mistakes tend to haunt us, especially when others remind us of them.

Forgiving self is one of life's greatest challenges. It is made easier when those who love us have forgiven us and when we base our lives on God's grace, not our own goodness. Someone said, "Grace means there is nothing I can ever do to make God love me more, and nothing I can ever do to make God love me less." When we accept our own imperfections, then we become candidates for grace. And we find it easier to offer grace to others, even to your dad (who should have never sent you to second base).

For Reflection and Discussion

• Why are we so hard on ourselves? Is it poor self-image, unrealistic expectations or what?
• Does forgiving the guilty party then make it easier for them to forgive themselves?

Scripture: "And be kind to one another, tenderhearted, forgiving one another, as God in Christ has forgiven you" (Ephesians 4:32).

Prayer: "Lord, when I sin I am harder on myself than I should be. I'm also tough on myself when I mess up in sports. I know that you forgive me, but forgiving myself is my greatest challenge. Amen."

Backspace

Those who keep the books for baseball games know that each player is assigned a number. For example, the pitcher is one, catcher is two, etc. The third baseman is five. If the third baseman makes an error in a game, it is recorded, "E5."

Chipper Jones, Braves third baseman, made an admission several years ago of an extra-marital affair and believe me, it shocked the Atlanta area. Headlines and talk shows screamed the news about fallen heroes and celebrity temptations. Hmm. Something must be in the water. We are not surprised any more when we hear about politicians, athletes, prominent preachers and just plain ol' folk like you and me, who fail to live up to expectations. Mortals. Mortals who sin. Dr. Jekyll becomes Mr. Hyde.

Chipper reportedly said, "In life there aren't any mulligans." To the uninitiated, a mulligan is golf lingo for "a second chance." When you hit a bad shot, you get

---

Are the expectations for Christians so high that none of us can keep them?

---

to do it over. Most golfers, by the way, only allow a mulligan on the first tee. True, we can't undo what has been done. We can't unring a bell that has been rung or undo the damage a sin has caused.

In 1906, a man named Elmer Beehler invented the backspace on the typewriter. (A typewriter, by the way, was an ancient writing device used last century. The backspace allowed the user to redo a mistake.) Since none of us type perfectly and all of our lives are flawed, we all could use Beehler's backspace. I'm sure Chipper and lots of others would like to undo what has been done. In the manuscript that is our lives, a backspace can never fully atone.

Thanks to God, though, that forgiveness is available and with God's help, we can rewrite the story of our lives. Each of our stories can have a different ending if shaped by the Master's hand.

For Reflection and Discussion

• Are the expectations for Christians so high that none of us can keep them?
• Do we hold celebrities to higher standards and if so, why?
• How do we overcome our failures and go on to re-build our lives?

Scripture: "For all have sinned and fallen short of the glory of God" (Romans 3:23).

Prayer: "Eternal God, each of us fails everyday in some way to live up to the calling of being a Christian. We don't want to underestimate the impact of our failures or to downplay them in any way, yet at the same time, we want to overcome them and move on with our lives. We need your strength and grace to do so. Amen."

The Golden Rule

Next time you attend a major league baseball game, notice that fans are led in the singing of "Take Me Out to the Ballgame" during the seventh-inning stretch. Thousands of fans rise to their feet in the middle of the seventh, stretch and sing the theme song for America's pastime. The song ends with the familiar words: "For it's one, two, three strikes you're out at the old ballgame."

Some youth parents in Cherokee County, Georgia, have given new meaning to the word "strikes." It seems a fight broke out between two coaches and seven parents after a baseball game between two teams of 10-year olds. The problems began when a grandfather of one of the players yelled a racial slur at one of the assistant coaches and then began taunting the father of one of the opposing team members. Tempers flared. Punches were thrown. (This is a far cry from "Root, root, root

---

We teach the Golden Rule to our kids, but didn't Jesus give it to a group of adults?

---

for the home team.") A witness said that "a mother got out of her car and hit a guy over the head with a water bottle." (Whatever happened to "Buy me some peanuts and Cracker Jacks"?) The two head coaches were banished from the league for the year and seven parents, including the grandfather, were banished for life.

So much is being said about today's young people in light of all the school shootings. "What's wrong with our youth?" is the cry heard 'round America. Well, maybe, just maybe they need some better role models.

Of this incident someone said, "The poor kids were not involved. It was the stupid adults." We teach the Golden Rule to our kids, but didn't Jesus give it to a group of adults?

For Reflection and Discussion

• Is competition always healthy? Why is it that competition can cause us to do things that we might otherwise not do?
• What would be appropriate ways to express anger in the heat of competition?
• Why are parents so intent on their kids winning and succeeding in sports?
• Do sports occupy too significant a place in our culture?

Scripture: "Be angry, and yet do not sin..." (Ephesians 4:26).

Prayer: "Lord, I want to win, but I also want to be a good sport, win or lose. Help me to enjoy sports without worshipping them. May my Christian faith always find a way to shine through in the heat of competition. Amen."

A Coach's Kid

His name is Drew Fowlkes, and he hit the ever-loving daylights out of a baseball. The fact that it was in the bottom of the last inning to win the game made it really special. Considering it was a high school state playoff game made it even more special. And since our son Tyler is on the team and I got to watch every heart-stopping second of it – that made it incredible for me. And what made it "out of this world" was that I got to see his dad immediately after the game. And oh, did I tell you, his dad is a college baseball coach? The smile on dad's face after the game was as wide as A-Rod's bank account. That smile was as wide as from here to Cooperstown, which by the way, is about where that homer landed. You have never seen a prouder daddy than I saw after Drew hit "the shot heard 'round town."

I got to thinking about coaches' kids and preachers' kids. I got to thinking about how there are some kids who can have unusual burdens and expectations placed on them by their parents and by others. I'm sure there are coaches' kids who hate the game of baseball because

---

He wants us to make Him proud with how we live and how we play the game of life.

---

the game has been pushed on them by mom or dad or the expectations from others were too great. There are preachers' kids who hate the church because the expectations were too much or the kid saw how the church tore up dad or the family. Drew seems to really love the game, which speaks highly of his family.

It's great to see kids make mom and dad proud. It is even better to see kids play the game for the love of the game.

I believe that God is in some ways, as Jesus said, like a father, and I also believe that He is in many ways, like a coach. He wants us to make Him proud with how we live and how we play the game of life. The expectations He has for us are not over-bearing but simply reflective of our talents and interests – just like a dad and just like a coach.

For Reflection and Discussion

• What are the expectations placed upon you by your parents and others? Are they too much?
• Do you feel extra pressure to perform because of these expectations?
• What do you believe God wants from you?

Scripture: "And, fathers, do not provoke your children to anger; but bring them up in the discipline and instruction of the Lord" (Ephesians 6:4).

Prayer: "Father, I know that you expect a lot from me as a Christian. Sometimes I feel pressure to perform in sports and life because of the expectations from parents and coaches. Help me to strive for high, but realistic goals. Amen."

Baseball

Ted Terrific

Watching the Major League Baseball All-Star Game is a Davis ritual. I have never been so moved by a baseball game as I was during the '99 classic. I hope you got to watch it. The American League won the game, but it was the pre-game show that stole all the attention.

The game was played in legendary Fenway Park in Boston. After the players were introduced to thunderous applause, they remained on the field as Ted Williams, Red Sox legend, was introduced. As perhaps the game's greatest hitter of all time and the last to hit .400 in a season (.406 in '41), otherwise known as the Splendid Splinter or Teddy Ballgame, Williams has earned his place as a baseball icon. He was a two-time Triple Crown winner, a feat almost unheard of in today's game. You could feel the ovation jumping out of the TV screen as he rode on a golf cart to the pitcher's mound. About 80 years of age and recovering from a recent stroke, Williams still loved to talk about baseball.

A most amazing and touching scene developed. All the current All-Stars gathered around the master just to shake his hand and hear his words of advice. Tears

---

You and I must sit at the feet of Jesus and learn more about the "game of life."

---

rolled down Williams' face as he talked about the game he loved, and the current millionaire stars shared the same emotion. They were taking in every word that fell from his lips.

I couldn't help but think about Jesus and his disciples. Disciples are learners – those who sit at the feet of the Master. Even major leaguers must continue to listen and learn.

You and I must sit at the feet of Jesus and learn more about the "game of life." When our hitting is in a "slump," we should read the instruction book. When we commit an "error," we must look to the Master for reproof and direction.

For Reflection and Discussion

• Who are your sports heroes and why?
• What is the greatest sports tip and spiritual tip that you have ever received?
• In what areas of life do you have the most discipline and in what areas do you need work?

Scripture: "Take my yoke upon you, and learn from me…" (Matthew 11:29).

Prayer: "Almighty God, sometimes I don't take the time or make the effort to be the best athlete or coach that I can be. At other times, my commitment to Christ is also lacking, and I fail to practice the basics of my faith that I know would make me a better Christian. Forgive me. Amen."

Copycats

I like Bowdon, Georgia, a small community some ten miles west of us. Nice town. But I hadn't planned to spend the day there. But one Saturday, several years ago, I did. Arriving around 12:15 p.m. at the baseball fields, we departed those same fields at 10:30 p.m. Now that's a day full of coaching and watching baseball. The fact that the team our son, Tyler, plays on, won the tournament made it a very enjoyable, but long day.

So when the last out was made and our team ran jubilantly from the field, Tyler and his friend Cal ran straight for the dugout. While other kids shouted for joy and "high-fived" one another, those two headed straight

---

Parents, your children are watching and mimicking you. Before God, make sure you are setting a good example.

---

for the Gatorade container. Thirsty? No, no, no. They picked it up to douse our head coach, Cal's dad.

I know our son watches too much ESPN, and this incident only confirms it. Our house looks like a shrine to SportsCenter. We have a life size cut-out of Chris Berman sitting in the recliner. Tyler has seen for years on ESPN video clips of players on the winning team pouring the sports drink on the head of the shocked coach. I don't know whose brilliant idea that was – probably some Gatorade salesman, but I think it needs a decent burial. Enough is enough.

My take on all this is that children emulate what they see, on TV, at the movies and in the home. They are great copycats. Imitators. Parrots. Parents, your children are watching and mimicking you. Before God, make sure you are setting a good example.

Sports provide some wonderful instruction for kids about hard work, discipline, fundamentals and teamwork. I'm not convinced, however, that dousing the coach with a cold drink is one of them!

For Reflection and Discussion

• What are some things you have seen kids do to mimic adults?
• How do we have some control over the media's influence upon our children?

Scripture: "Finally, brethren...whatsoever is pure...think on these things" (Philippians 4:8).

Prayer: "Father, I know that the things we put into our minds have either a positive or negative effect. Help me to use good judgment about what I watch and read so that my mind will be filled with good images that would honor you. Amen."

Single Sermon

A baseball tournament several years ago with Tyler's team in Clearwater, Florida brought this story. Our team, composed of some rather small and frail looking 11-year olds, was facing a 12-year-old team that looked like a bunch of Neanderthals. 'Nuff said. They were big and strong and we were overmatched. We hung tough, however, and were down only 6-3 in the last inning. We've got the bases loaded and two outs. We're talking high drama here.

Tyler's friend, Chase, is at the plate facing a pitcher that looked to be a cross between Nolan Ryan and The Incredible Hulk. 'Bout seven feet tall. He had one eye right in the middle of his forehead. Snorting. Grunting. Foaming at the mouth. Throwing fast balls that looked like BBs. There were two strikes on Chase before you could say "Attaboy." We were down to our last strike.

We may feel like grasshoppers compared to the giant problems that confront us daily.

Chase fouls off strike three. Fouls off another. And another. And another. Finally, he got one he could hit and sent a single up the middle. Though we lost the game, it was the best "at bat" I saw in the whole tournament. What a great piece of hitting with the game on the line.

You may face pitchers like that everyday. Marital problems? Huge. Finances? Mammoth. Temptation? Frightening. I recall that the Hebrew children in the wilderness saw the giants in the Promised Land and said, "...we seemed like grasshoppers" (Numbers 13:33).

We all face obstacles that, at the time, seem a whole lot bigger than our Little League selves. We may feel like grasshoppers compared to the giant problems that confront us daily. Hang in there with faith in God. Grit your teeth and before long you'll get something you can handle.

For Reflection and Discussion

• In the face of mounting obstacles, how do we not panic, but keep our focus on the Lord?
• Why does faith in God seem to come so easily for some and so hard for others?

Scripture: "Be strong and courageous; do not be frightened or dismayed, for the Lord your God is with you wherever you go" (Joshua 1:9).

Prayer: "Almighty God, I sometimes have a difficult time having faith that you will see me through my difficulties. I take my eyes off of you and put them on my problems. Help me to trust you on a daily basis. Amen."

A Goat and a Curse

I'm beginning to believe it. What about you? I mean, how else can one explain the events at the ol' ballpark? I stayed up late several nights back in '03 to cheer on the Cubs in hopes of warding off the curse that has plagued them since before I was born. We Braves fans think we have it bad for winning all those division titles in a row and "only" one World Series. Consider the plight of the poor Cubs before you bemoan the fall collapse of our local team. At least the Braves aren't cursed. (They aren't are they?) The Cubs on the other hand have had the "curse of the goat" since the 1940s when a man named Sam Gianis took a billy goat to a Cubs game

---

Is it true that God will never give us more than we can handle?

---

and was unceremoniously kicked out. He cursed the Cubs and said they would never win a World Series until a goat was brought back to Wrigley Field.

So what do you think? Are you a believer in curses? The writer of Deuteronomy believed in them, stating on several occasions that those who follow the ways of the Lord will be blessed and those who don't will be cursed (chapter 28). He said that blessings and curses were to be understood in terms of land, crops, offspring, and health.

It seems to me that this Deuteronomic theology falls far short of New Testament faith. I only wish that theology and baseball could be that simple. For example, we all know dear saints of God who endure hardship after hardship, and conversely we know ungodly folk who enjoy great blessings.

Baseball is the same. The failure of the Cubs can't be blamed on a curse, but rather on bad clutch pitching and hitting. You are cursed only if you think you are. Maybe some baseball fans in those cities believe in such nonsense. Likewise, it is nonsense to believe that those who follow the Lord will only know "health and wealth," as some like to preach. In fact, Jesus called on his followers to carry a cross and he taught that the "last shall be first and the first shall be last" (Matthew 19:30). Under that arrangement, maybe the Cubs are winners after all.

For Reflection and Discussion

• Is it true that God will never give us more than we can handle?
• Does God send bad things our way or do we simply live in a world of accidents, germs, and diseases?
• How do I take the bad that has happened and learn from it without becoming bitter about life and mad at God?

Scripture: "We know that all things work together for good for those who love God…" (Romans 8:28).

Prayer: "Lord, sometimes when bad things happen I get discouraged and think that I can't handle it. May I become stronger through my trials and learn valuable life lessons along the way. Amen"

Heavenly Hall

Ruth, Gehrig, Cobb, Musial, DiMaggio, Mays, Mantle, and Davis. I'm talking about Hall of Fame names. Ones that are household names. Sure-fire, first-round ballot inductees into Cooperstown. I mean, they've all got the stats to show for it – home runs and RBIs.

Okay, the first seven names do, but Davis? Do I have delusions of adequacy? Am I a legend in my own mind? Well, I did play Little League baseball, but truthfully I spent more time on the bench than on base. Actually the Hall of Fame of which I speak has nothing to do with baseball, but with building.

A few years ago, my dad was inducted into the Dothan, Alabama, area Home Builders Hall of Fame. It was quite an honor for him and for our family. That's the closest I will ever get to any Hall of Fame, unless there is one for geezer dads with the youngest child. (I'm now

---

One only receives an award after death if one did something worthy of it in life.

55, with a 5-year old.)   Abraham and I are on a short list. Like I said, Dad's induction was quite an honor. The presenter read a list of dad's accomplishments, not only as a builder, but in the community. The award he received is called a posthumous one, an award presented after death. One only receives an award after death if one did something worthy of it in life.

Hebrews chapter 11 presents the Faith Hall of Fame. Familiar names, all of them: Abraham, Sarah, Jacob, Joseph, Rahab, David, to name a few. What were their qualifications for induction? They were men and women of faith, who were willing to serve God no matter the circumstances. And most of them never got their rewards in this life; some in fact labored in relative obscurity. Hebrews 12:1 describes them as a great "cloud of witnesses." They all made it into God's Hall of Fame and now they wait on our induction.

Do you have the stats?

For Reflection and Discussion

• What are the most important things in God's Kingdom, attitudes or actions?
• What should be our motivation for serving Christ – heaven and its rewards or simply God's love in our hearts?
• How much does the praise of others mean to you in your sports and in life?

Scripture: "For all of us must appear before the judgment seat of Christ, so that we may receive recompense for what has been done in the body, whether good or evil" (2 Corinthians 5:10).

Prayer: "Lord, I must admit that I enjoy the attention that comes from success in sports, but I would like for my success to honor you. Grant that I can play the game and live my life out of love for others and you and not for some reward that I might receive. Amen."

Reflections on Ted and Tug

I am penning this story in the winter of '04 and maybe you missed this baseball note in your sports section – the death of Phillies reliever, Tug McGraw. He was a colorful character who is remembered by many for leaping off the mound after recording the last out of the '80 World Series in which the Phillies beat Kansas City. He is also remembered for his classic quote after the '73 series, in which he was asked how he would spend his World Series share. He said: "Ninety percent I'll spend on good times, women, and Irish whiskey. The other ten per cent I'll probably waste." Tug McGraw died in 2004 after a long battle fighting a malignant brain tumor.

And that brings us to Ted. Ted McCollum, friend and fellow minister also recently succumbed to a brain

---

What Ted will be remembered for were his tireless efforts on behalf of the "have-nots" of our community.

---

tumor. Ted and Tug both loved life. Both were fine athletes. Ted, an avid golfer, shot a 78 in his last round, while battling a brain tumor. Oh, by the way, did I mention, he was 70 years of age? Darn impressive!

I can't say for sure how Ted would have spent a World Series share, but I do know how he spent his life. He spent his life in service to God and others. His legacy will be more than his exploits on the links. Ted will be remembered for his tireless efforts on behalf of the "have-nots" of our community. His work for local ministries like the Emergency Shelter for battered women, the Soup Kitchen for the hungry, Interfaith clothing for the poor and the Transient Fund for those passing through our community, will have an impact for years to come. Those four ministries make for a grand slam. Thanks, Ted.

For Reflection and Discussion

• How do you want to be remembered? Are you doing things that will have a lasting impact, long after your death?
• Sports are important to us, but can we sometimes lose perspective on the importance of games versus real life issues?

Scripture: "Let your light shine before others, so that they may see your good works and give glory to your Father in heaven" (Matthew 5:16).

Prayer: "Father, sometimes I get caught up in my sports so much that I forget how temporary they are. I want to make my life count for things that are eternal and that will have a lasting effect on this earth. Forgive me for being short-sighted and give me a vision of the good that I can do for others. Amen."

"SRO"

I hadn't been to an Atlanta Braves game in a couple of years, so I thought "Why not?" Why not go with the church group and take Sheri, Natalie, and Tyler? After all, Natalie, our little girl loves baseball; in fact, it's about all she has ever known. What none of us knew is that it would be the largest Braves crowd of the year, and we heard the dreaded words at the ticket booth: Sold Out. However, there were "Standing Room Only" tickets and so we gobbled those up. When they say SRO, they mean it. You can only stand in designated spots, behind a rope and lots of people.

The church group split up, with the Davises left to cope with our then 1-year old. We stood behind lots of tomahawk-chopping Braves' fans hoping for a glimpse of the action on the field. About the third inning, out of frustration because we couldn't see, we wound up in "Tooner Field," a place inside the stadium for kids,

---

Church should be different. When you worship it is not about you. It is about God.

---

complete with a Cartoon Network movie. For the adults there is a TV screen showing the Braves game. Natalie watched a movie and I watched the game on TV. Let's see. We spent $20 on tickets to the game, $10 to park, $10 on refreshments and who knows what on gas for the car, all so that I could watch the game on TV! What is wrong with this picture?

I got to thinking about SRO. We have it at church. Ever heard of Easter? What is the difference in a Braves game and Sunday morning worship? Why not SRO every Sunday morning? For sure, the Braves game is entertainment. From the time you pay for the ticket and walk in the gate, you are entertained. You sit and watch as a spectator and cheer or boo if you like. But nothing is expected of you or demanded of you.

Church should be different. When you worship, it is not about you. It is about God. Something should be demanded of you and expected of you. You can be in the presence of Chipper Jones or any other sports star and not be changed, but to be in the presence of God: Now that is something. I hope the reason we don't have SRO every Sunday is because something is demanded of you at church. Some people don't want that. Fine. But if you really want to get in the game of life and be challenged, then see you Sunday at the church of your choice. But come ready to play, not watch.

For Reflection and Discussion

• We live in an entertainment age and some people go to church expecting to be entertained. Do you?
• Are you more committed to your church or to your sports?

Scripture: "But strive first for the kingdom of God and His righteousness, and all these things will be given to you as well" (Matthew 6:33).

Prayer: "Lord, I fail to give to my church my fullest attention and my talents. Forgive me for putting sports ahead of church, and give me the strength to support my church in every way that I can. Amen."

Torn Between Two (or Three) Lovers

When I was a kid, I pulled for the New York Yankees. There, I have said it, and I feel better already. I can explain. You see, this was pre-George Steinbrenner and every kid my age idolized Mickey Mantle. So, I did have reasons and I defend to this day my love, as a kid, for the Bronx Bombers. Now I hate them. And boy does it feel good.

Truth is, as a kid I grew out of my love for the Yankees and developed one for the St. Louis Cardinals. One of my brothers got me interested, and once I listened to the radio broadcast in those days on KMOX radio out of St.

Where and when does our commitment to sports get in the way of our faith?

Louis, with Jack Buck and Harry Caray doing the play by play, I was hooked. In high school, while my friends were out on dates, I sat in my driveway and listened to the call of the game by that legendary radio team. (This explains why I was 35 when I got married.)

I remained an avid Cardinal fan, but when we moved to Houston, Texas, I got caught up in the local team. The Astros had Nolan Ryan and good teams in those years, and so my allegiance changed a bit.

Then we moved to Georgia and I immediately identified with the local team, the Braves. And so I have become an ardent Braves fan, tomahawk-chopping enough to throw out an elbow.

Adding to the mix is my most recent allegiance and interest, the Boston Red Sox. We visited Boston a few years ago and fell in love with the place. We took the subway out to Fenway Park even though it was the baseball off-season, just to be able to say we had been there and walked around the stadium. (Sheri loved that part of our vacation.) Besides, pulling for the under-dog is the American way.

Boy, did I ever have a dilemma back in the '97 World Series. Should I pull for the Cardinals, whom I have loved for years, or my newest love, the downtrodden Sox? I don't think I am fickle. But rather, I have the capacity to love several teams at once. Where am I going with all this baseball stuff? Allegiance! I simply ask you to consider where your priorities will be and where your ultimate allegiance will fall.

For Reflection and Discussion

• Jesus seemed to demand total allegiance from his followers. Does He demand that from us too?
• Where and when does our commitment to sports get in the way of our faith?

Scripture: "Choose you this day whom you will serve…but as for me and my household, we will serve the Lord" (Joshua 24:15).

Prayer: "Father, there are so many things, some of them good, that demand my time and attention. Sports are a good thing, but sometimes they get in the way of my allegiance to Christ and the church. Amen."

Chapter Two

Basketball

Not Like Mike

Perhaps you saw the Nike commercials several years ago that featured the Chicago Bulls superstar Michael Jordan, in which we were implored to "Be like Mike." Easier said than done. Recently for Father's Day, Sheri and Tyler gave me some new Nike Air Jordan basketball shoes. I suppose that in a perfect world, one could put on these shoes and "be like Mike." I tried – laced them up and went to the backyard with Tyler, intent on flying to the hoop like Mike. After a running start I took off from the free throw line, hoping to get airborne and then rattle the rim with a resounding dunk. (Ha!) Well, I

Living with limitations is what we all have to do sooner or later.

---

took off from the free throw line and…landed on the free throw line. Shades of Humpty Dumpty and the Hindenberg. I was airborne about $1/1000^{th}$ as long as the Wright brothers' first flight. I learned quickly that having Michael's shoes does not make me "like Mike."

Facing the facts is tough. I'm not a NBA player. I'm not even a good church league basketball player anymore. Kids in the neighborhood go easy on me.

Tyler and I play H-O-R-S-E in the backyard and he spots me the H-O-R-S.

Living with limitations is what we all have to do sooner or later. I wish I could turn back the clock...but, on the other hand, I kinda like me the way I am. With limitations. Weaknesses. Warts and all.

The apostle Paul said he had "learned to be content." So have I. If it's okay with you, instead of being "like Mike," I'll just be "like me."

For Reflection and Discussion

• Why do some parents have a hard time accepting their declining skills and thus, try to relive their sports glory through their kids?
• How can we be content as players with the limited skills that we do have and not try to be or do something we can't?
• How do we, on the one hand, have sports heroes, but on the other hand live with the reality that we probably won't ever attain the sports success that they have?

Scripture: "For I have learned to be content with whatever I have" (Philippians 4:11).

Prayer: "Almighty God, I know that I have limitations in my sports abilities and yet, I want to be the best that I can be. Grant that I will be content with who I am and with the talent or lack of talent that I have. Help me to play and coach sports for the love of the game. Amen."

Move Over J.J.

J.J. Redick of Duke University was/is renowned as a free throw shooter. He led the nation in free throw percentage and he is the NCAA all-time leader in three-point shots. In his Duke career he made 91.1 per cent or 660 out of 724 free throws.

But, move over J.J. As good as you are, there is a girl who is better. Deb is better. That is Deb Remmerde of Northwestern College, who, back in '06, set the all-time record for free throws made in a row in competition – 133. When I say all-time, I mean all-time. She not only set the NAIA record, but broke the NCAA record of 94 set by some guy named Paul Claxton and the NBA record of 94 set by Michael Williams.

Deb is described by friends as a "gym rat" and someone who prefers "shooting drills to media thrills." By the way, during this current streak, one of her shots actually

---

The disciplines of worship, Bible study, fellowship, stewardship and prayer are like two dribbles and a shot.

---

hit the rim and fell in. The crowd gasped. To Deb this streak is nothing. She once made 485 in a row on the goal at the family farm. For the record, I once made 10 in a row in the backyard. Eight hit the rim. I would have made 485 in a row, but I got distracted by something. Maybe it was the dog or the wind, or whatever.

Deb attributes her success to following a routine. Discipline. She says, "I try to do everything the same way every time I step to the line. I use the same routine, take two dribbles and shoot it."

When we get "fouled" by others or when stuff happens, I wonder how much better we would fare if we had the routines down. The disciplines of worship, Bible study, fellowship, stewardship and prayer are like two dribbles and a shot.

For Reflection and Discussion

• What are the disciplines that make you the coach or player that you are or hope to become?
• Why do you have discipline in your sports life but not in your spiritual life?
• What are the most important disciplines for the Christian and why?

Scripture: "...discipline yourself for the purpose of godliness" (1 Timothy 4:7).

Prayer: "Father, grant that I may take my spiritual life as seriously as I do my sports life. And help me to take the time to work on the basics of my relationship with you. Amen."

"Hotter than a Pistol"

It was the most amazing video I have seen since the baseball bounced off Jose Canseco's head (admittedly, a hard surface) and over the fence for a home-run. What video? Jason McElwain's. Jason is the team manager for the Greece Athena High School basketball team in Greece, New York. As manager, he keeps the stats and hands out water bottles. The 17-year-old senior usually sits on the bench in a shirt and tie. Jason, 5 feet 6 inches, was considered too small to make the junior varsity last year, so he joined the team as a manager, staying near the sport he loves.

Oh, and did I tell you that Jason is autistic? Jason's dad said he has always worried that his son would get a technical foul from the bench, by becoming too

---

Why do you think God has such concern for people that the Bible calls "the least of these"?

---

emotional and out of control. Guess what happened on February 15, 2006? Did he get a technical? No. He got in a game. And did he ever get in the game. Late in the game, with his team way ahead, the coach pointed at him to enter the contest. A crowd favorite, Jason entered the game and the crowd went bonkers.

And guess what? A miracle happened. I've seen the video. Too bad there wasn't video of the Red Sea crossing. I'm telling you, Jason was Moses. Jason hit six three-point shots (his last five in a row, including one at the buzzer) and finished with 20 points. He was carried off the court on his teammates' shoulders. When reporters stuck microphones in his face for post-game comments, he did his best Michael Jordan impersonation and said, "I was hotter than a pistol."

I don't know much about autism, but I do know something about basketball. And the story brought me to tears. His coach said, "It was as touching as any moment I have ever had in sports." Thanks to the coach for taking one of "the least of these," the poor, the outcast, the naked, the hungry, the autistic, and putting him in the game.

I've always said that if the Bible were being written today, instead of "The Lord is my shepherd," it would be "The Lord is my coach." Thank you coach, for putting Jason in the game.

For Reflection and Discussion

• Do you know someone like Jason who needs your love and attention?
• Why do you think God has such concern for people whom the Bible calls "the least of these"?

Scripture: "Truly I say to you, to the extent that you did it to one of these my brothers, even the least of these, you did it unto me" (Matthew 25:40).

Prayer: "Lord, help us to care for everyone on our team, our coaches, managers, and players. And give us a heart of compassion for those associated with our team who are less fortunate. Amen."

Walking and Chewing Gum

I got a frantic call from our son Tyler one day, about one hour before a basketball game. The heel on one of his basketball shoes had torn loose and he needed some new ones - and quick. "Size 11s, black and white Nike," were his instructions. So, I hurried to the shoe store and found just that. The salesman said "I'll give you a deal on these" (always hold your breath when you hear those words), as he put them in the box. I rushed them to the gym and much to Tyler's surprise, we discovered the reason for the "deal." Two left shoes. I'm not kidding. What really bothers me about this story is that there is someone in town walking around or playing ball wearing two right shoes.

When a person is a real klutz, we say things like, "He can't walk and chew gum at the same time" or "He's got

---

Many people are just as gifted, but their talents aren't as easily seen or appreciated.

---

two left feet." Well, if you know someone with two left feet, tell him we know a store that will give him "a great deal."

There are, of course, people who have absolutely no coordination and aren't any good at sports. However, some of those same people can blow a trumpet or play a piano like a pro. Or they can teach a Sunday school class like an All-Star. Some can paint like Picasso. Others can deal in the business world like Donald Trump.

We all have talents that are gifts from God. Some talents are obvious, such as sports stars that can throw, run or dunk. Many people are just as gifted, but their talents aren't as easily seen or appreciated. ·For example, churches are filled with people whose ministry is cooking casseroles for the sick or whose talent is making strangers feel welcome at church. Some folk may not be "stars" in your eyes, but they are in God's.

For Reflection and Discussion

• Don't we tend to elevate people with sports talent and overlook others who are equally talented in other areas?
• Do you know some really talented people in your church or on your team who don't get the recognition they deserve?

Scripture: "Now there are varieties of gifts, but the same Spirit. And there are varieties of ministries, and the same Lord" (1 Corinthians 12: 4-5).

Prayer: "Lord, I want to use my talents for your glory and not for my own. Also, I ask you to help me to appreciate and respect others, who are equally talented, just in other areas. Amen."

Letting Go and Going On

I don't know where you were in January of '99, but in case you missed it, two basketball players announced their retirement: (1) Michael Jordan retired (the first time) from the NBA as the greatest player ever and (2) I retired from church league basketball. Michael's press conference was attended by hundreds and watched by millions around the world. I held a press conference in my study attended by none.

Michael Jordan retired with six championship rings, five league MVPs and ten scoring titles. I won no titles or MVPs and I believe my final averages were three points, four rebounds and five turnovers per game. Jordan

---

There comes a time in life when we must move on to something else - to new games and new adventures.

---

made the final shot of his career to win the NBA championship over the Utah Jazz. My last game was a church league one in which I limped off the court with a pulled calf muscle. Two points. Michael waited seven months after his last game to retire. I waited two years. Michael and I have a lot in common.

Seriously, there is one bit of common ground (or hardwood). We both love the game. I'd rather play basketball than eat, sleep, or preach. I've played on real basketball teams, intramural teams, and backyard hoops all my life. To walk away from it or anything we love is tough. I realize that my days of playing competitively are over and a part of me dies in letting it go. I would still love to take the court against the young guys. My heart says "yes" but my body says "no." There comes a time in life when we must move on to something else – to new games and new adventures. (Shuffleboard anyone?)

Gotta let go sometime. What about you? Hanging on or letting go?

For Reflection and Discussion

• Why is it so difficult for adults to accept each phase of life and to be content with the limitations that they bring?
• Why do we choose to live in the past instead of focusing more on the present and future?

Scripture: "For everything there is a season, and a time for every matter under heaven…a time to seek, and a time to lose" (Ecclesiastes 3:1, 6).

Prayer: "Father, I tend to live too much in the past, choosing to think about the 'good ol' days' instead of looking ahead to all the great things that you have in store for me. May I accept my current stage of life with grace and embrace it. Amen."

Coach's Corner

Shock. Anguish. Disbelief. Angst. All these feelings belong to a coach (me). I'm writing this column immediately after our son's 7/8-year-old team's last basketball game. Will someone please kick me if I ever agree to coach again?

As you can tell, we lost the game. It's not so much that we lost, but how we lost. We were leading 10-5, (that's right, 10-5. These are little kids, remember?), with a

---

Maybe you feel down and out and wonder if you will ever see the light of day.

---

minute-and-a-half left in the game. I thought the game was over. Our opponents had only scored five points the entire game. How could they score five in the last minute-and-a-half? Well, they did. I'll spare you the details. We lost 11-10 in overtime and I have a sick feeling in my stomach. Oh, by the way, this was the championship game for the season-ending tournament. I'm sick.

In the words of Yogi Berra: "It ain't over till it's over." I thought it was over. Our opponents didn't. They never quit. Could there be some personal, spiritual application here? Maybe you feel down and out and wonder if you will ever see the light of day. There seem to be so many people in our society who are under a heavy load with overbearing circumstances. Depression for some. Despair for others.

If these words describe you, please don't ever give up. Victory can be snatched from the "jaws of defeat." The

Christian story is all about life coming out of death. Hope from despair. Three-pointers to win ballgames. In the words of Anthony Campollo, "It's Friday, but Sunday's coming."

For Reflection and Discussion

• Have you ever won a game in the final minutes, a game that seemed all but lost?
• Are you ever tempted to give up on sports or life because you seem so far behind and think that you will never catch up or overcome the deficit?

Scripture: "Therefore, my beloved, be steadfast, immovable, always excelling in the work of the Lord, because you know that in the Lord your labor is not in vain" (1 Corinthians 15:58).

Prayer: "Lord, I am so tempted to quit when things don't go my way or when I feel overwhelmed. Give me courage to persevere and remind me always that the work I do for the team or for you is not in vain. And may I always be quick to praise you for the strength I receive. Amen."

Hoop Homily

Are you looking for a sign that the Apocalypse is upon us? How about this news item? In 1962, an otherwise meaningless NBA game between the Philadelphia Warriors and the New York Knicks, became one of its greatest. That was the game in which Philadelphia star Wilt Chamberlian scored 100 points. That record still stands as the highest scoring game ever by an individual, and it may never be broken. And now this: The basketball that Wilt Chamberlain used to score a record 100 points was auctioned for $551,844.

Some people have more money than brains. I mean, would you pay half-a-million dollars for a basketball?

Aren't our values all fouled up? Where we spend our money tells us what we value.

(And there's some dispute as to whether this is actually "the" ball.) I'd pay about $10-$20 for that basketball. To score 100 points in a game is beyond description, but it was by an extraordinary player with an ordinary basketball. By the way, my point totals for my church league and intramural league careers might total 100. I could play basketball in the backyard by myself for hours and not score 100 points.

This story reminds me of the man who broke into the department store one night and switched all the price tags. When the store opened the next day, someone bought a new suit for $25, men's cologne for $500, etc. Aren't our values all fouled up? Our values are expressed not by what we say, but by what we do. We say we value old people, but not for more than an hour or two at a time. We say compassion is a value we possess, but we seem to have more for trapped whales than for the homeless in the streets of our richest cities. We say we value God, but how many attend church regularly?

Where we spend our money and how much tells us what we value. What do you value? Look at your checkbook and it will contain a clear account of what is really important to you. It tells the story of our lives.

I'm sure not going to spend mine on a Wilt Chamberlain basketball.

For Reflection and Discussion

• What price tag would you put on your sports career? Church life? Family life?
• How important are things to you, versus the value of loved ones and teammates?

Scripture: "For where your treasure is, there your heart will be also" (Matthew 6:21).

Prayer: "Almighty God, I say that I value family and teammates more than possessions, but I don't live like I do. Sometimes I wonder if my priorities are way off base. Forgive me for spending too much time on things that don't have lasting value. Amen."

MJ and Me

The media was parked outside our home (108 Lisa Lane) all that week (October, 2001). They bombarded me with questions every time I left the house. "Now that Michael Jordan is making his comeback, are you, too, coming out of retirement?" Believe me, it was tempting. I think of all my great hoops accomplishments: '75 college intramural champs, '77 seminary champs, '99 neighborhood H-O-R-S-E champion. The list goes on and on.

Should I come back? I heard the naysayers. "It's been 20 years since he was in his prime." "That was 30

For the Christian, the best is yet to come. God has new and exciting things for us, no matter our age.

---

pounds ago." "Arthritic knees and pulled muscles; surely he's a step slower." My fans (Sheri and Tyler) wanted me to stay retired, and besides, they said, my comeback would detract from Michael's. So, upon further review, I decided to stay in the rocking chair and just re-live my past glory.

Michael Jordan said that he was playing again "for the love of the game." I hope that was the case. For the Christian, we don't live in the past or try to relive past accomplishments. For the Christian, the best is yet to come. God has new and exciting things for us, no matter our age.

Moses was 80 years old when he got the call to lead his people out of Egypt. I'm sure some of the Hebrews wondered, "Does he still have it?" "Can he hit the jumper?" "I'll bet he is a step slow for Pharaoh's chariots." Thank goodness Moses had his eyes gazing squarely into the future. The "Promised Land" is always out in front of us, never behind us.

For Reflection and Discussion

• How much faith do you have that God has great plans for your life?
• Do you think that God has exhausted all his blessings for you in the past or is the best yet to come?
• Are you stuck spiritually and emotionally in the past or are you living each day in the present tense?

Scripture: "Eye hath not seen, nor ear heard, nor the heart conceived, what God has prepared for those who love him" (1 Corinthians 2:9).

Prayer: "Lord, I want so much to believe that you have great plans for my life, but sometimes my faith wavers. Help me to look ahead and dream big. Give me the strength to let go of the past and to believe in you and pursue my dreams. Amen."

Sarah's Story

I don't normally cry at breakfast. Sheri's a good cook and even on her bad days there is nothing so bad as to evoke tears. Speaking of bad cooking, I did recently burn a Pop Tart. Burn it? No, scorched it. It caught fire in the toaster! "Dad, why is one side of the Pop Tart dark?" "Chocolate, son, chocolate."

But normally, I don't cry at breakfast. That is, until last week. Sheri and Tyler had left for school, and I did the morning ritual of reading the paper and drinking my coffee. My day doesn't start without them. That's when I read about Sarah Wolfe, 17-year-old Decatur High student, who died of cancer. An all "A" student, she played flute in the band and ran cross-country. She was an incredibly outgoing young lady who cheered people

---

"It was hard to think about basketball...It was like basketball was not really as important."

---

up with her charm, wit and grace. Lots of friends. Said her dad, "I thought there would be a couple of close friends who would hang with this, but every time in the hospital, I'd have to be a traffic cop. And they were comfortable. They would hold the vomit bowl, clean it up and hold her hand." (That's when I began to weep.)

Decatur High boys basketball team dedicated their state tournament games to her. One of the basketball players, David Harbin, had known Sarah since kindergarten. He lamented after visiting her, "It scared me a little. It was hard to think about basketball when there's something that sad. It was like basketball was not really as important."

Basketball's March Madness has begun as I write this article. I love it. Can't wait. I will watch every game I possibly can. But, when I do, I'll think about Sarah and remember, "It's just a game." There will be lots of standing ovations for basketball players and teams in the weeks ahead, but none will compare to the one given to Sarah by her church in January after her last round of chemo. And the church's ovation won't compare to the "standing o'" reserved for her in Heaven.

For Reflection and Discussion

• Who are some inspirational people that have touched your life?
• Is there someone you know who is suffering like Sarah, that as a Christian and friend, you could help?

Scripture: "Bear one another's burdens, and in this way you will fulfill the law of Christ" (Galatians 6:2).

Prayer: "Father, I am afraid to help others because sometimes I don't know what to do or say. Give me courage to help others who suffer. Also, help me to remember that my sports life is 'just a game.' Amen."

March Madness

So how are your picks going? Mine? Not so well. I'm talking about the NCAA basketball tournament and my annual attempt to pick the winners. Our Minister of Music, our son Tyler, and I pick them every year and the winner gets a free meal from The Varsity, Atlanta's favorite fast-food restaurant, courtesy of the other two. Once again Tyler has won and I have finished third. Obviously I'm not much at predicting the future. Don't look for Steve's Palm Reading and Crystal Ball Shop to be opening in your neighborhood anytime soon.

On the other hand, I'm not as bad as some throughout history. For example, the President of an equipment company said in 1977, "There is no reason for any individual to have a computer in their home." In 1962, someone from a record company said of the Beatles, "We don't like their sound." The President of a Michigan bank said to Henry Ford's lawyer in 1903, "The horse is here to stay, but the automobile is only a novelty, a fad."

Well, you get the point. We humans more often than not

Although trusting Jesus does not remove us from the contingencies of life, we are assured that He is with us.

---

have missed our guesses about the future. But we should not despair because we trust a Savior who gives us the power to cope with the unexpected, the "upsets," if you will. Life is very much like the NCAA tourney, full of the unthinkable and unpredictable. Although trusting Jesus does not remove us from the contingencies of life, we are assured that He is with us and that "all things work together for good to those who love God" (Romans 8:28). I'll wager a Varsity hotdog on that!

For Reflection and Discussion

• How do we put our faith in God when there are so many contingencies, germs, accidents and diseases in our world?
• How much freedom do I have in determining my future, and what do I do when I make a bad decision?
• Is God's will for my life set in stone or is there flexibility to account for my weaknesses and poor choices?

Scripture: "Trust in the Lord with all your heart, and do not rely on your own insight. In all your ways acknowledge Him, and He shall direct your paths" (Proverbs 3:5-6).

Prayer: "Lord, to think about my future is scary because I make mistakes and sometimes make bad choices. In spite of that, guide my life that I might do your will in all things. Amen."

"Hey, Coach"

My main assignment on a mission trip a few years ago to Virginia was to head up the sports camp. One of the churches that we assisted used the sports camp as an outreach tool, and a very successful one at that. There were about 50 children all total who participated, with 22 being prospects for the church. Tyler, our son, and I taught basketball for three fifty-minute sessions daily.

Several things in my life recently have reminded me that "spring chicken" is not a term that anyone in their right mind would use to describe me, at this stage of life. Chasing a 7-month old around the house, aching knees and an affinity for John Wayne movies are some of these things. Teaching at the sports camp only reinforced the conviction that my best days, sports-wise, are behind me; thus the phrase "over the hill" might be a better description.

There was a precious and precocious third-grade girl in our basketball camp. Her name was Erin. She beat me twice in free throw competition. Twice. She's a third-grader, for heaven's sake. Both times she made three

---

A good coach and a good minister will give credit where it is due. And that would be to our God, who gives us the victory.

---

out of five free throws. I made ... uh, fewer than three. Despite the blow to my already battered ego, the sports camp experience was a good one for me. I loved being called "coach" all week. "Hey coach, show me how to dribble." "Hey coach, I'm tired." Trying to coach for only a week gives me an even greater appreciation for those who do it for a living.

I've always suspected that coaches and ministers have much in common. Coaches teach and so do ministers. I like teaching, whether it is the Bible or how to shoot a free throw (my recent experience not withstanding). I also suspect that ministers and coaches get way too much credit when things go well and way too much blame when things don't. A good coach and a good minister will give credit where it is due. And that would be to our God, who gives us the victory.

For Reflection and Discussion

• As a player, how can you be more supportive of your coaches and honor them for their hard work on your behalf?
• What is the toughest aspect of coaching, handling defeat or handling the criticism from parents?
• As a coach, is it hard to give the glory to God when you have worked so hard to achieve results?

Scripture: "So, whether you eat or drink, or whatever you do, do everything for the glory of God" (1 Corinthians 10:31).

Prayer: "Father, I work so hard to help kids and then get criticized no matter what decision I make. Give me grace to handle adversity and humility to praise you when things go well. Amen."

Chapter Three

Football

"Are You Ready for Some Football?"

It's that time of year again. My favorite. I love the fall of the year because of the weather and the pigskin. I love football: high school, college, and pro. Especially college.

Football fever is catching on at our house. A few days ago Tyler made a goal post (3-feet-high) out of cardboard. We taped it to the inside of the front window in the living room and proceeded to kick a plastic peewee football at it. We were having quite a game until an errant kick clipped a leaf off an African violet in

---

Moderation is a good word for all of us to hear.

---

the windowsill. I thought a sacrificial leaf was a small price to pay for the guys' pigskin pleasure. Sheri thought otherwise. The goal post was moved to a more appropriate place in the stadium (house).

I'm not the best husband in the world during football season. You know, the couch potato syndrome sets in. Let's see, there is a Friday night high school game, Saturday college, Sunday pro, Monday Night Football, and now even a Thursday night college game. What a menu for someone with a football feeding frenzy! And I'm not good at dieting. Putting down the remote during football season is as difficult as passing on homemade peach ice cream. What to do?

Ours is an addicted society: drugs, money, tobacco, sex, power, TV, and football. Some might say that our addiction to football (and other sports) is as destructive to the family as these others. Lots of men (and women too) neglect their families because the remote control controls them. I struggle like a lot of you do with my commitments to being a good husband, father and pastor versus other things that would take my time and attention. Moderation is a good word for all of us to hear. The Bible calls it "self-control" (Gal. 5:23).

For Reflection and Discussion

• When does our devotion to sports become a problem?
• How can we become as obsessed with the things of God as we are with sports?
• What if we spent as much time on spiritual things as we do practicing our sport?

Scripture: "You must make every effort to support your faith with goodness, and goodness with knowledge, and knowledge with self-control" (1 Peter 1:5-6).

Prayer: "Father, I have a tendency to be easily addicted to things, in particular, sports. Give me the strength to say 'no' to misplaced priorities and to say 'yes' to the things that are eternal. Amen."

Wheelchair Witness

Maybe you didn't notice the small announcement on your local sports page. It was way too small considering the enormity of its content. Like I said, you may not have even noticed. I noticed because it was about Darryl Stingley's death, and I will never forget him or "that play."

That play was when Stingley, who was a wide receiver for the New England Patriots, was tackled hard by Jack Tatum of the Oakland Raiders back in 1978. I remember it like it was yesterday, because Stingley didn't get up. He couldn't. He was paralyzed and would remain that way for the next 29 years. An autopsy revealed that he died from the aftereffects of the injuries suffered in that fateful football collision.

I have always been touched by Stingley's response to his injuries and some of his quotes resurfaced after his death. In a 1988 interview he said, "I have relived that moment over and over again. I was 26-years old at the

---

The "Why me, Why this, and Why now?" questions are natural, but not productive.

---

time, and I remember thinking, 'What's going to happen to me? If I live, what am I going to be like? And then there were all those whys, whys, whys?'" Then he added these powerful words, "It was only after I stopped asking why, that I was able to regroup and go on with my life."

Someone said that time heals all wounds. Nope. Sorry. With time, some people become more bitter and angry and have the disposition of a piece of burnt toast. Do you know people like that? It is so easy to get stuck emotionally, mentally and spiritually because of some traumatic experience, some "tough hit" that we took. The "Why me, Why this, and Why now?" questions are natural, but not productive.

Stingley could finally get unstuck only when he quit asking those questions and learned to accept what had happened to him. Are you stuck in the past? Do you constantly hit "play" and "rewind" on the tape (CD) that is your life. Stop. It does no good. That's what Darryl would say.

For Reflection and Discussion

• Do you constantly beat yourself up over something that happened in the past?
• Do you fret over mistakes you make in sports? If so, how can you move past that?

Scripture: "Beloved, I do not consider that I have made it my own, but this one thing I do; forgetting what lies behind and reaching forward to what lies ahead, I press on toward the goal" (Philippians 3:13-14).

Prayer: "Almighty God, I trust that you have the power to take my mistakes and bring good out of them. Give me the strength to forget what I have done or what has been done to me and give me the grace to look ahead. Amen."

Football

Birds or Broncos?

In 1998 our son Tyler was a fan of the Green Bay Packers all year. All year . . . that is until the Super Bowl. Something happened at halftime of that year's clash between Green Bay and Denver. With Denver leading, Tyler suddenly dropped the Packers like a hot potato (or was it Wisconsin cheese?) and became a vocal, ardent Broncos fan. "Dad, I've always liked Denver, too," he reasoned. "Son, you are what we call a 'fair-weather fan.' You should stick to one team, win or lose," I explained.

This year ('99), before the season started, I told Tyler that I'm a Falcons (our local team) fan and the birds

---

I've been trying to teach him about commitment. Pick your team and stick with them.

---

would be in the Super Bowl! Honest I did. Sheri is my witness. But the truth is, I was just kidding him. I didn't really believe it. I said, "Son, when the Falcons go to the Super Bowl, you can't pull for them because you're a Broncos fan." Lo and behold, it's the Birds and Broncos in THE GAME. Guess who Tyler is pulling for? Falcons! He switched again. He switches teams like Elizabeth Taylor (or Britney Spears) does husbands.

I've been trying to teach him about commitment. Pick your team and stick with them. "For better or worse, in sickness and in health," the marriage vows say. Our culture has difficulty with commitment because some view it as the enemy of freedom, spontaneity and "fun." Americans don't like the feeling of being restricted, thus we aren't good at making and keeping commitments.

Hosea said that Israel's love was like "the morning dew" (6:4), there for a brief moment and then vanquished by the sun.

Fumbles? Interceptions? Penalties? No problem. We're with you all the way. Go Falcons!

P S: The Falcons got hammered by the Broncos in the Super Bowl but I stuck with the locals 'till the bitter end.

For Reflection and Discussion

• How important is it to you to honor your commitments?
• Are you loyal to your team and teammates? Does loyalty extend to all your relationships?
• Does God's faithfulness to you inspire you also to be faithful to others?

Scripture: "For I desire steadfast love and not sacrifice" (Hosea 6:6).

Prayer: "Father, I am easily swayed and sometimes my loyalty is not what I want it to be. Forgive me and help me to be faithful to you and to other people in my life, including my players and teammates. I desire to have the 'steadfast love' that Hosea talks about. Amen."

Leonard's Winners

I'd rather watch college football than _____. OK, you fill in the blank. For me that's easy ("anything" is the correct answer) since it's one of my favorite things. Why do I like it so much? Part of the attraction is the sights and sounds. Fall is in the air. Marching bands. Rivalries. And Leonard's Losers. Leonard's Losers?

Only the college football faithful would have paid attention to the recent obituary. For many years a radio program hosted by "Leonard" Postero picked the losers in upcoming college football games. That's right, he picked the losers.   He added some southern humor and

---

A vital part of "training up a child" is to give them the data they will need for success.

---

had his own nicknames for each team. For example, the Georgia Bulldogs were the "red clay hounds" and the Florida Gators were the "giant water lizards." Said his widow, Elke, "The main thing was, not having to be correct, but to put a smile on somebody's face." I'm going to miss Leonard. He passed away recently from congestive heart failure in Athens, Georgia, and left behind a pigskin legacy.

A lot of people are losers because someone significant in their lives has told them they are. I don't claim to be a prognosticator (Nostradamus, I am not), but I think I could accurately predict what most kids will become by listening to what their significant others say about them. "Son, you're a loser." Chances are he will be.

A vital part of "training up a child" is to give them the data they will need for success. In life as in football, there are winners and losers. Apparently, Leonard Postero was a winner in life, described by his wife as a caring and kind man. "If somebody needed a tooth filled, or a child needed surgery and Leonard knew about it, he would take care of it," Elke said. He is survived by three daughters and two sons. I'd be willing to bet they are winners, just like Leonard.

For Reflection and Discussion

• How much are you doing to encourage your teammates and/or players to help them have confidence in their abilities?
• How do you overcome the negative comments from parents and continue to believe in yourself when others don't?

Scripture: "But encourage one another day after day…" (Hebrews 3:13).

Prayer: "Lord, forgive me when I am critical of my teammates or coaches and give me the grace to be positive and encouraging to others. May I be the kind of teammate and friend who lifts others up with my words. Amen."

Fourth and Long

John Elway is a future NFL Hall of Famer. But as a family man he was headed straight for the Hall of Shame. Since retirement a few years ago, the Denver Broncos #7 has been on the losing end of several scores. First, his dad died. Many business ventures got "sacked." His wife left him. Then, his twin sister died of lung cancer. Elway was king of the comebacks as a player, but this was fourth down and a country mile to go. And this was a real life battle, not a game.

When Janet, his wife of 18 years, walked out and took the kids, Elway was jolted into reality. He had neglected his wife and family for all these years, and he

---

Run the race. Play the game.
And don't quit on your family.

---

knew it. He hadn't been to a mall in 16 years. (Lucky guy!) He had never taken his family to an amusement park.

Said Elway: "Them leaving kind of woke me up. It was like a two-by-four to the heart." He changed. He went to the mall with Janet. Sent roses. Opened car doors. Played with the kids. The family was back together as quickly as you could say "Ready. Set. Hut."

Said Rick Reilly of *Sports Illustrated*, "Sometimes you think you have to be a god when all you really need to be is human." Amen.

Take a Knee

(The sad sequel to this story is that John and Janet Elway separated in 2002 and divorced in 2003. Sometimes we wait too long to make changes.)

I wonder how many of us try to be a superstar quarterback when all our spouse and kids need is a third-string right tackle. They need someone who will show up for practice, play hard and not quit when the going gets tough. In the words of the writer of Hebrews, "...let us run with patience the race that is set before us" (12:1). Run the race. Play the game. And don't quit on your family.

For Reflection and Discussion

• Do we have to be perfect as ballplayers, coaches or as parents to be successful?
• Is it difficult to balance your commitment to sports and your commitment to family? If so, why and what can you do to correct it?

Scripture: "Love...bears all things, believes all things, hopes all things, endures all things. Love never fails..." (1 Corinthians 13:4-8).

Prayer: "Father, my family life is not as great as it needs to be because sometimes I don't pay attention to their needs. I am too focused on my needs and not theirs. Forgive me. Amen."

Driver Training

Donald Driver stole cars as a seventh grader in Houston, Texas. He says the easiest ones to steal were old Cadillacs. Within thirty seconds he could smash a window, his right fist wrapped in a T-shirt, and be ready to roll, though he could barely see over the steering wheel. "I could drive pretty good," Driver was quoted as saying in a recent *Sports Illustrated* article. He stole twenty or thirty cars and only had to jump out once.

But oh that once. He stole the car and heard the police sirens. Flying down the street, he T-boned an old

---

"Why do you do this, young man? You could be doing so much more." The words stayed with him.

---

woman's car as she backed out of her driveway. He jumped out of the stolen car, but for some reason he checked on the old woman. "Go sit on my porch," she said, as the cops approached. For some strange reason, he trusted her. When the cops arrived, one inquired, "Who's that on your porch swing?" "Oh, that's my grandson," she said. After the police left, she scolded him, "Why do you do this, young man? You could be doing so much more with your life!"

Her kindness changed Donald Driver's life. Not instantly. But her act of kindness grew on him like kudzu on a Georgia pine – a little bit every day. "You could be doing so much more." The words stayed with him.

Driver is a starting wide receiver for the Green Bay packers and just signed a five-year contract worth $11.5

million. The Packers' community relations person said of Driver: "He's a wonderful man. He's always smiling, fun, and positive. He calls *me* up and asks if there are any (public relations) appearances I need done." He's made about 300 of those and all honorariums go to the Donald Driver Foundation, which helps needy people.

And the old lady with the porch swing in Houston? Oh, she is doing fine. And whenever Donald Driver is in that big city, he drops by to see her and thank her for an act of kindness years ago that changed his life.

For Reflection and Discussion

• Has anyone done a kind deed or offered kind words that made a difference in your life?
• How might a little kindness from you affect your team and players?

Scripture: "And be ye kind to one another, tender-hearted, forgiving one another" (Ephesians 4:32).

Prayer: "Father, thank you for the kindness of others who have encouraged me over the years. Help me to see the power of my words as I share them with my teammates and coaches. May I be a blessing to others by my words and deeds. Amen."

WWSD

David Brooks doesn't need my advice, but I give it to him anyway. David is the Offensive Coordinator for one of our local high school football teams and a member of our church. In other words, on Friday nights he calls the plays and fans like me sit in the stands and question his calls. He has forgotten more football than I have ever known.

When I say I question his calls, I'm teasing. On Friday nights, when he has run the ball a lot, I have yelled, "Throw the ball, Brooks." People in the stands almost always want the home team to throw it more. After one game, when the local team threw it a lot, he asked me with a smile on his face as wide as a goal post, "Did I throw it enough for you?" I responded with, "Coach, you threw it way too much tonight. Next time, keep it on the ground." You can never please the fickle fans.

We all try to teach our teenagers not to listen to the crowd, but to go with their own convictions.

I've even told David that I want his cell number so that I can call during the game and offer my expert advice. Well, the last thing David needs during the heat of battle and the last thing on his mind is WWSD (What Would Steve Do?). Truth is, I love football, but I had better stick to what I know, things like theology and how to hit a three iron.

We are all better off if we don't base our decisions on what others want us to do. An Offensive Coordinator had better have his convictions and game plan in place and not listen to his knucklehead minister, who knows more about "grace, love, and peace" than he does "ready, set, hut." We all try to teach our teenagers not to listen to the crowd, but to go with their own convictions. In other words, don't live your life trying to please the folk in the stands, but rather live it based on what you think your Father in heaven would want you to do. Now that is a game plan that will work. WWJD is much better than WWSD.

For Reflection and Discussion

• What areas of life are most difficult when it comes to peer pressure?
• Are significant decisions in your life based on what you think God wants you to do or what you feel would be the most popular thing to do?

Scripture: "And do not be conformed to this world, but be transformed by the renewing of your mind, that you may prove what the will of God is, that which is good and acceptable and perfect" (Romans 12:2).

Prayer: "Father, I acknowledge that I am often influenced by the crowd. I listen to what my friends are saying I ought to do instead of listening to what I know you want me to do. It is so easy to be influenced by others because I want to be liked and popular. Please give me the strength and courage of my convictions. Amen."

Chapter Four

Golf

Moe the Schmoe

He died on September 4, 2004, and it hardly got a line on the Sports page. He being Moe Norman, the eccentric and often misunderstood Canadian golfer. Who was Moe Norman? Just the best striker of the golf ball who ever lived, according to Sam Snead, Lee Trevino, Vijah Singh and countless others. He was, plain and simply, the most accurate golfer on the planet. Not the longest hitter or the best putter–he found putting to be boring–but the straightest hitter ever. He once

---

Is it right as a Christian to make fun of people who have odd personalities?

---

went eleven years, about 230,000 golf shots, without hitting one out-of-bounds. He hit 356 drives off a standard wooden tee without disturbing it from the ground. Someone said that is like saying that you swatted at flies and never missed. But was he any good? In his 50 years as a professional in Canada, he had 17 holes-in-one, nine double-eagles, won over 50 tournaments and set more than 30 course records. He shot 59 three times, once when he was 62.

And so, how is it that you have never heard of him? How is it that he labored in relative obscurity for all those years? Friends and physicians felt that Norman was probably an *autistic savant*, a term used for autistics that have exceptional math, memory, or music skills. A misfit? Yes. He was deathly afraid of strangers and could not handle the stress of having to speak in public after winning a tournament. Idiosyncrasies? Yes. He drank 24 Cokes a day and never had a credit card or a date in his life. Moe wore three watches on his left arm, all set to the same time. Moe's photographic memory made him a master at playing cards. Did you ever see the movie *Rainman*, starring Dustin Hoffman, as a middle-aged autistic man? Those who knew him said, "That's Moe."

What a shame that we don't try to understand people like Moe better and try to find what makes them tick. What would Jesus do on the "links" of life?

For Reflection and Discussion

• Do you know people who are different and who are often misunderstood?
• Is it right as a Christian to make fun of people who have odd personalities?
• How did Jesus treat people like Moe?

Scripture: "Do not judge lest you be judged yourself" (Matthew 7:1).

Prayer: "Lord, I sometimes prejudge others based on their appearance or personality. Forgive me and help me to have compassion for all of your children. Amen."

Brotherhood

I love golf. I've loved it all my life. I've had more fun times on the golf course and had more laughs than anyone could imagine. I've laughed so hard I cried when a friend would hit a gosh-awful shot or someone would tell a golf joke. I don't remember ever crying on the course, though sometimes I felt like it after totaling my score. I have shed a few, however, when watching on TV or reading about the game I love.

One story moved me to tears. It was about veteran golfer Ben Crenshaw and his long-time caddie, Carl Jackson. Jackson, who knows Augusta National like I know my way around a baptistry, has caddied for

---

"He was standing there when I needed him. That's a brother. That's someone who loves me."

Crenshaw there for 30 years. They are as different as, well, black and white. Crenshaw is white and Jackson is black. Crenshaw is a Texan from the country club scene and Jackson, an Augusta native, took up caddying because he didn't want to work in the cotton fields.

Like I said, Jackson has been Crenshaw's caddie for 30 Masters, but not back in 2000. You see, that was the year Carl Jackson heard the dreaded "c" word. At the age of 46, he was diagnosed with colon cancer. There was a new treatment that would help, but it was too expensive. At that time, Jackson said, "Let me go, instead of running up a big bill my family was going to have to pay." A few minutes later, the phone was ringing. Crenshaw was calling from Texas, with a

Texas-sized heart, saying, do whatever it takes to get well. He said he would cover the bills.

Said Carl Jackson: "He was standing there when I needed him. That's a brother. That's someone who loves me." Carl is now cancer free. He is also free to love in return. Said the caddie of the golfer, "Silver and gold, I have none, but I'll give him what I've got."

For Reflection and Discussion

• I'm just wondering how grateful are we for those special people that God has put in our lives?
• And how do we show our gratitude? Do you have any "brothers" like Crenshaw and what will you do for them?
• What as Christians should we do to foster better race relations?

Scripture: "But there is a friend who sticks closer than a brother" (Proverbs 18:24).

Prayer: "Lord, thank you for those who give so much to help me as a coach, parent and friend. I thank you for the generosity of others and the goodness in them. Help me to be kind to others, all others, from all races and walks of life. Amen."

"Fore"

Golf is not exactly a contact sport, like say, football and rugby. In football, players often sprain ankles, dislocate shoulders and tear up knees. In golf, the only "contact" is when the club meets the ball or in the case of a fit of rage, club meets tree. That's why you don't see ambulances hauling golfers off the course or see trainers taping up knees after a golfer makes a double-bogey. "How was your round?" "OK, except I tore an ACL and dislocated my shoulder." You don't hear that kind of talk from golfers. Golfers' injuries are usually a strained back or a bruised ego.

I read a few years ago that actor Matt Damon took a"crack" at learning to play golf and "cracked" his ribs instead. The actor was learning to play the game for an

---

Golf's not nearly as easy as it looks...Following Christ isn't as easy as it might appear to some.

---

upcoming movie when he swung so hard at the ball that he swung himself right into the doctor's office. The film's director had told Damon, that with computer graphics, they could either make him look like a golfer or he could try to learn the game himself. He tried. Golf's not nearly as easy as it looks, a painful lesson for an actor or would-be golfer.

Just as an actor can't act like a golfer, you and I aren't in the business of Christian theatrics. Following Christ isn't as easy as it might appear to some, but we don't need to depend on computer graphics to help us imitate Christ. Let's take discipleship up ourselves. See you at church Sunday, cracked ribs and all. That's par for the course.

For Reflection and Discussion

• What is the toughest part about being a Christian?
• Do you know Christians who have suffered hardships because of their deep commitment to Christ?
• Are we raising a generation of Christians who have been sheltered and pampered to the point that they will falter when the going gets tough?

Scripture: "If any want to become my followers, let them deny themselves and take up their cross and follow me. For those who want to save their life will lose it, and those who lose their life for my sake, and for the sake of the gospel, will save it" (Mark 8:34).

Prayer: "Lord, sometimes my Christian walk is way too easy. I'm not challenged to live the authentic Christian life, but rather I just go along with the crowd. I know very little about denying myself anything, much less about carrying a cross. Help me to be more determined about my faith. Amen."

Amen Corner

I become the world's sorriest husband during Masters weekend. The other 51 weekends of the year I'm in the bottom five percent, but when the cameras are on the Augusta National, I sink even lower. Sheri asks, "Honey, will you take out the garbage that you promised you would take out last fall?" "No, dear, Tiger is teeing off in an hour and I don't want to miss it." I don't miss a shot unless the house is burning down.

It is every golfer's dream to play Augusta National before taking that great golf cart ride in the sky. Perhaps the most famous section of the course is what's called "Amen Corner," holes 11-13. The phrase was first coined in a 1958 *Sports Illustrated* article written by

---

We all have sacred places, whether at church on "your" pew or a special place in your home, like the back porch.

Herbert Warren Wind, who was searching for an appropriate name for that critical stretch of the course. He got the name from an old jazz recording, "Shouting at Amen Corner."

Where is your "Amen Corner?" Perhaps it is a place, a sacred place, filled with azaleas, dogwoods and loblolly pines, which make Augusta National so special. We all have sacred places, whether at church on "your" pew or a special place in your home, like the back porch. Some places are so special we find it easy to utter "Amen."

Perhaps for others, "Amen Corner" is a time of testing in life when all seems to be fraught with danger (water hazards, sand traps and slick greens). If you have ever watched the professionals play holes 11-13 at Augusta National, then you know of what I speak. But, in the midst of all the knee-knocking perils that make you hesitant to even draw back the club, you say "Amen." In spite of the hardships and obstacles, somehow and someway, you say it. And you say it with great courage and conviction. "Amen!" "And all God's chillin' (pros and amateurs) said Amen!"

For Reflection and Discussion

• Do you have special places where you study and pray, places where you find it easier to talk to and experience God?
• And what about when life gets tough? Can you say "Amen" in the midst of life's greatest challenges?

Scripture: "Do not lag in zeal, be ardent in spirit, serve the Lord. Rejoice in hope, be patient in suffering, persevere in prayer" (Romans 12:11-12).

Prayer: "Father, thank you for special places where it is easy to worship you and pray to you. Enable me to do that also in places where it is not easy and at times when life is difficult and challenging. Amen."

Links Lagniappe

I've never seen an angel (except Sheri). At least not that I know. Wouldn't know what one looks like, unless of course, it comes with wings and a halo. So, I'm not sure what shape, size and brand they come in. Are they 75 years of age, pudgy, with a Pennsylvania accent? Possibly.

I was hitting golf balls at a driving range recently. My golf game has been non-existent because of a newborn named Natalie and weather named Wicked.   So I went

---

Have you met an angel lately or better still, have you been one to someone else?

---

out on the first warm day in a blue moon to see if I knew which end of the club to hold.   The results were mediocre at best. Army golf – left, right, left, right. No good.

Enter my angel – my 75-year-old, pudgy angel. He was watching me hit and a brief conversation ensued. Come to find out he is a teaching pro, so I asked for his observations about my swing. He proceeded to drop manna from heaven. "Take it straight down the line," he said. "Drop it in the slot." (Golf lingo.) Magic. Pure magic. I started grooving shots the way I know I can. Felt great! Move over Tiger Woods. (Well, let's not get carried away.)

I asked him his name, fully expecting him to say "Gabriel." "Tony," he said. Tony? An angel named Tony? Oh well. They come in all shapes, sizes and names, I suppose. Have you met an angel lately, or better still, have you been one to someone else?

For Reflection and Discussion

• Who is that special someone, friend, family or stranger, who gave you some unforgettable words of wisdom?
• Do you have a special someone, who from time to time, offers words of encouragement?
• Are you being an angel to others, by offering encouragement and showing them the way to God?

Scripture: "Do not neglect to show hospitality to strangers, for by doing that some have entertained angels without knowing it" (Hebrews 13:2).

Prayer: "Lord, thank you for the special people that you have sent my way to encourage me – coaches, family and friends. I pray that I might be that kind of person to others, the kind of person who lifts others up; not the kind who tears others down. May I never underestimate the impact I can have on others. Amen."

Keeping Score

I recently took our four-year old, at her request, to the golf course to play a few holes. I just happened, by the way, to shoot my best nine-hole score of all time. In fact, bring on Tiger Woods, because it just happened to be the best front-side score in history. Oh, and did I tell you, Natalie kept score. She gave me scores of one, two and three on every hole but one, where she gave me a four. I believe my nine-hole score was a 22. I like the way she keeps score.

On the first hole, she told me not to hit it in the forest. I then promptly hit the first shot into the woods, or forest, as she called it. (It didn't matter though, because she gave me a two on the scorecard for that hole.) I liked her approach to sand traps. She saw them as opportunities for fun and play instead of hazards that are

---

There are some things in life to worry about, but none of them are on the golf course.

---

to be avoided. On the greens, she seemed not to care whether it took her two putts or 22 to get the ball in the cup. And water hazards were an opportunity to watch the ducks instead of bringing angst.

Her attitude of just having fun seemed to rub off on me, as I seemed to care less whether I hit it crooked or not, or whether I one-putted or three-putted. For most of my life I have taken the game way too seriously, often awaking in the middle of the night with a nightmare about a flubbed shot or a vision about the correction of a swing flaw.

Having a four-year old who could care less about my slice into the forest is a wonderful reminder about the things that really matter in life. If I played golf for a living, then there is cause for concern when the ball doesn't go where it is supposed to go. But I don't. And playing the grand ol' game with my daughter is a reminder that (1) I am one lucky man, and (2) there are some things in life to worry about, but none of them are on the golf course.

For Reflection and Discussion

• Do you become so obsessed with your sport that you lose perspective?
• What things can you do away from the game to gain a better perspective?

Scripture: "Be anxious for nothing, but in everything by prayer and supplication with thanksgiving, let your requests be made known to God. And the peace of God, which surpasses all understanding, will guard your hearts and minds in Christ Jesus" (Philippians 4:6-7).

Prayer: "Lord, I tend to worry about things that don't matter, and I worry especially about my team's performance on the sports field. Help me to gain a healthy view of life that puts sports in the proper place. And may my faith be strong enough that your peace replaces worry. Amen."

Ryder or Wrong?

If you have no addictions, raise your hand and move to the head of the class. Let me jog your memory. Drugs? Alcohol? Chocolate? Shopping? Sex? TV? Hunting? Sports? OK, so maybe you have a few. Does spending three days on the couch glued to the TV constitute an addiction?

Every two years, I spend a couple of days in September watching the Ryder Cup. To the uninitiated, the Ryder

---

I guess most of us show where our treasure is by where our time is spent.

Cup is a golf match between the best U.S. pros and the best from Europe. I love it. I can't get enough of it. I'm hooked. I had to leave my perch on the couch for a while to pick up sticks in the yard. Can you say "sullen"? If Sheri said, "The house is on fire!" my response would be to call 911 – during a commercial.

During the Ryder Cup, I am a worse husband, father and pastor than normal. I tell my church members that when they pass away, try to avoid a weekend in September. Please. I am so focused on the golf I tend to ignore everything else. So, the Ryder Cup is my favorite golfing event to watch. Oh, by the way, America lost the most recent Cup. The Europeans whipped us on the links, and I'm not too happy about it.

Do you know what I wish? I wish I could say that I spent the weekend in prayer on my knees instead of on the couch watching golf. But I can't. Wouldn't it be great to be addicted to prayer? A knee-time instead of a t-time? Time with the "Master" instead of in front of the "Masters." I guess most of us show where our treasure is by where our time is spent. No heavenly crowns for me on Ryder Cup weekend. And no golden cup for the Americans. We both lost out.

For Reflection and Discussion

• What addictions do you have and what are you doing to overcome them?
• Addictions tend to take a drain on our spiritual lives. How are your addictions affecting your walk with God?

Scripture: "For there is no distinction, since all have sinned and fallen short of the glory of God" (Romans 3:22-23).

Prayer: "Master, I know that my addictions hurt my relationship with you. I am a sinner and in need of your grace. Help me to spend more time nourishing my spiritual life and less nourishing my sinful ways. Amen."

"Like Going to Church"

When Easter Sunday and Sunday of the Masters golf tournament are on the same day, I am one happy preacher. (It doesn't take much to make a preacher happy, except maybe a packed church and some donuts on Sunday morning.) Why? Because we have nothing at church on Easter afternoon or evening and I can turn into a Masters couch potato.

I read with great interest some comments made by Nick Faldo, three-time champion of the event. He is now a TV commentator for CBS and was asked about the tournament, now that he is up in the booth and not a competitor anymore. Being a TV commentator at Augusta can be hazardous to one's career, because Masters' officials have had two commentators dropped

---

I long for sacred places and sacred times that bring a sense of "the holy" into my life.

---

because of what they deemed as inappropriate comments about the course or fans. Faldo, who has a free-wheeling style in the broadcast booth, says he isn't worried about getting in trouble with the Masters' big-wigs. Said Faldo, "I'm very respectful of Augusta. This is a totally different place, like going to church, isn't it?"

Nick and I have the same attitude about church. Just as golfers have such great respect for those "holy grounds" at Augusta National, I like to see the same respect for things that are sacred. Augusta National is not like other golf courses and the Masters tournament is unlike any other. In a similar way, I want church to be different from what I experience the rest of the week. I need something to lift me above the mundane and average things in my world. I long for sacred places and sacred times that bring a sense of "the holy" into my life.

There is a trend today to build new churches that don't look like churches. The reasoning is that some people are intimidated by buildings with stained glass and arches. So, they build churches to look like office complexes. That is okay, but it's not for me. I want a church that looks and feels like a church. To use Faldo's words, I want "a totally different place."

For Reflection and Discussion

• Are there sacred places in sports, such as Wrigley Field and Cooperstown?
• What is it about church that is different and holy?
• Are there sacred places and sacred things in your life?

Scripture: "Remove the sandals from your feet, for the place on which you are standing is holy ground" (Exodus 3:5).

Prayer: "Father, I need to make church a special time and a special place. Help me to appreciate the sacredness of it and other places in my life as well. Amen."

Aces

I played the grand ol' game of golf for some 40 years before I had one. I hit a lot of good shots on par threes over that time, but one had never gone in for a hole-in-one, until a church tournament years ago, when one dropped in the cup for an ace. I danced and hollered like a Pentecostal preacher at a tent revival. I had lots of witnesses that day, thank goodness. Which reminds me of the minister who skipped church one Sunday to play golf. While playing a round by himself, he hit a hole-in-one. As the joke goes, God laughed from the heavens and said, "Who is he going to tell?" Well, like I said, I had witnesses. I've now had three and consider myself lucky.

But that is nothing compared to Jacqueline Gagne of Rancho Mirage, California, who has reportedly had 12 aces in a span of about six months. This is an unprecedented pace and she has her doubters (including

---

Do players and coaches exaggerate their skills and accomplishments?

---

me); some who think that the lady from Rancho Mirage is seeing "mirages." A Wall Street Journal article estimated the odds of having 10 (she's had 12) aces at 12 septillion to one. (It sounds like Jacqueline needs to be playing the lottery instead of the links.) Gagne's claim received some support recently, however, when a crew from a local TV station happened to capture one of the aces on camera.

It is too bad that we can't just accept someone's word. The lack of truth telling in our culture is appalling, whether it comes from Washington, or the state house or a neighbor down the street. How do we expect to take Jacqueline Gagne at her word when others in loftier positions of leadership can't be taken at theirs?

I am reminded of a football game in South Florida years ago, when in the closing seconds of a close game, the quarterback threw a beautiful pass to a wide-open receiver in the end zone. As the pass sailed through the night air, the lights went out in the stadium. They remained off for a matter of seconds. When they came back on, there was the receiver standing in the end zone holding the ball. Did he or didn't he? Too bad we can't just take him at his word.

For Reflection and Discussion

• What about truth telling in sports? Do players and coaches exaggerate their skills and accomplishments?
• How important is it in sports that you be able to trust your teammates?

Scripture: "But let your statement be 'Yes, yes' or 'no, no'; and anything beyond these is of evil" (Matthew 5:37).

Prayer: "Almighty God, help me to be honest about my ability in sports and truthful to my teammates and coaches. Forgive me when I don't tell the truth, whether out of fear or for personal gain. Amen."

Chapter Five

Catchall

(Wrestling, Bobsledding, Bicycling, Camping, ESPN, Boxing, Soccer, Horse Racing and Hockey)

"Uncle"

I love wrestling. Now before you drop your teeth and have a conniption fit, I don't mean WCW (World Championship Wrestling). The wrestling I'm talking about is the father/son type. Me (father). Tyler (son). Tyler is about 4 feet, 50 pounds. I'm about 6 feet and several more pounds than my son. I have a decided advantage when we wrestle, and I do my best Hulk Hogan impersonation and try to pummel the little whippersnapper. Recently, in one of our championship bouts, I had him in a vice grip (or was it a full nelson?) and he cried "Uncle."

"Uncle" is a synonym (why, I don't know) for "I give

Do you ever feel like the little kid who is having the tar beaten out of him by the neighborhood bully?

---

up." If you were the little guy with a big ol' daddy on top, you too might echo the words of the boxer Roberto Duran, *"No mas,"* when he was being pummeled by Sugar Ray Leonard in their 1980 rematch in New Orleans. *"No mas"* is "Uncle" in Spanish. "I give up. I've had enough."

Do you ever feel like the little kid who is having the tar beaten out of him by the neighborhood bully? Life becomes WCW played out in the ring that is our lives. There are some very wonderful people in my church and perhaps some on your team who have been battling tremendous odds. The big guy on top is cancer, divorce, unemployment or grief. I couldn't blame them if they cried "Uncle" a thousand times over. Could you?

Oh, I know the cliché, "Quitters never win, and winners never quit." But heck with clichés; this is real life stuff. I honestly don't know how some of them keep going, but they do.

For Reflection and Discussion

• As an athlete or coach, how do you not give up when the team is going bad or your own game is suffering?
• How can you be more sensitive to the off-the-field struggles of your players and coaches?

Scripture: "I can do all things through Christ who strengthens me" (Philippians 4:13).

Prayer: "Lord, sometimes I get caught up in my own world and don't pay attention to the struggles of others. Give me compassion for my teammates, players and coaches who have struggles, huge struggles, in every day life. Amen."

Solid Gold

Bobsledding was big in my hometown. Yeah buddy. Baseball or bobsledding? Tough choice for a little boy growing up in south Alabama. Should I pursue "America's pastime" and follow in the footsteps of Babe Ruth and Mickey Mantle or become a great bobsledder like...uh...well, other bobsledder legends. "Mom and dad, please don't make me play baseball. All my friends are bobsledders."

Seriously, how would someone from the sovereign state of Alabama ever, even in his/her wildest dreams, fathom the possibility? Meet Vonetta Flowers, from Helena,

---

Our Christian faith should form the backdrop for all our dreams...Most of us don't think big enough.

Alabama. She teamed with Jill Bakken of Utah to win the inaugural women's Olympic bobsled competition in 2002. Said Flowers: "This is a dream come true for me. I always wanted to compete in the Summer Olympics, but God had a different plan for me. I feel very blessed."

Isn't it great when dreams come true? All of our dreams should include a divine perspective. Our Christian faith should form the backdrop for all our dreams, as Vonetta's did. Most of us don't think big enough. Do you remember the powerful words of the British dramatist and journalist, George Bernard Shaw? He said: "Some men see things as they are, and ask, 'Why?' I dream dreams that never were, and ask, 'Why not?'"

A book written years ago, *Your God Is Too Small,* comes to mind. Do we really believe that God could do great things for our lives, church, and community? Why don't you ask a young lady from Alabama who dreamed of bobsledding gold.

For Reflection and Discussion

• What are your dreams for yourself and your team? Have you dreamed big enough?
• What do you do when dreams and reality don't match? How do you recover to dream again?
• Are you inspired more by what is out in front of you in the future or by what is in your past?

Scripture: "Where there is no vision, the people perish" (Proverbs 29:18).

Prayer: "Almighty God, help me to dream big and then work hard to achieve them. May my goals always be meshed with those of my team. Amen."

No "Plain O'" from Plano

So what's the big deal? I can do the same thing he does.
I'll admit I haven't done it in years, but they say that
once you have, you never forget. I'm talking about
riding a bicycle like this Lance Armstrong dude. The
fact that the Tour-de-Georgia came down our street and
Lance, yes *the* Lance Armstrong, pedaled past the
church has become big local news. So what is the big
deal? I can ride a bike, and, in fact, when I was twenty-
five years old, I was a better cyclist than Lance. Of
course, he was only six at the time.

Seriously, I have great respect for what this courageous
man from Plano, Texas has accomplished. Overcoming
cancer is enough to garner adulation, but to win (now)
seven straight Tour de France races is phenomenal.
Like so many others that day, I stood on the sidewalk in
front of the church and took pictures as they flew (or
pedaled) past. But that pack of bikers was moving so
fast, I doubt I got a good one. By the way, did anyone
tell Lance about the speed limit on our local streets?

The speed with which Lance and the others raced past
our church has become a life lesson of sorts. Lance, join

**Are you too busy with your sports to be a good and
faithful church member?**

---

the crowd. Did you know that only about fifteen percent
of the good folk in our county attend church, any
church, on any given Sunday? And about one in three
have church membership in any church. So, they aren't
just pedaling past our church, but all churches.

So why don't they stop and come in for a visit? Lance had a good excuse; he was in a race. But so are they. Wrong kind though – rat race. Literally thousands of people drive (or should I say race?) past our church every day and many are in too big a hurry to notice our beautiful facilities, or better yet, come inside to worship. What a shame. So here is the question of the day: What can we do, if anything, to entice a water break at church for life's weary bikers?

For Reflection and Discussion

• Are you too busy with your sports to be a good and faithful church member?
• How can you be a better witness for Christ to your teammates or players and encourage them to be active in a local church?

Scripture: "Let us consider how to stimulate one another to love and good deeds, not forsaking the assembling of ourselves together" (Hebrews 10:24-25).

Prayer: "Father, I am afraid sometimes to talk about my faith. Give me courage to be a good witness and may a significant part of my witness be my faithfulness to my local church. Help those who work so faithfully at my church and thank you for them. Amen."

Camping In

It's the "out" part that I don't like. Camping out has never been my favorite thing to do. In fact, it has never made my top one thousand. Camping out ranks right ahead of hang-gliding and parachuting. I did try camping a couple of times as a kid, only because our church had the boys/fathers group go to the woods and do their best Davy Crockett impersonation. As I recall, he died at the Alamo, and I thought I would suffer a similar fate camping out.

Someone told me that research shows that families who camp together, stay together. My reaction? So what? I'm not camping out even if research shows that it promotes world peace and will usher in the Kingdom. I just don't like to camp out. All of which brings me to the recent church outing where some of the fine young dads in our church took some of the boys to a local state park to "you know what." As they were leaving the

---

Do you take time to see the handiwork of God in nature? And if so, does it draw you closer to Him?

---

church parking lot and talking about the menu for the evening (hot dogs cooked on the grill), one of the dads said he was going to pick up some BBQ ribs on the way. BBQ ribs? Hey, I might reconsider this whole camping experience. When I was a kid, ribs were never on the camping menu. It made me wonder if the dads were also taking foam mattresses and fans. How about a nightlight and a CD player?

In my more honest moments (and this happens to be one, so please take note), I confess that outdoor experiences with nature are good things. Most of mine are limited to golf and baseball, but I know that communing with God's beautiful creation can be a very enriching and spiritual experience. It can bring a peace of mind that one can't get in the city and a perspective on life that we often lose sight of in our self-centered worlds. To spend time in God's beautiful, natural world inspired the words of the Psalmist, "When I look at thy heavens, the work of thy fingers...what is man that thou art mindful of him, and the son of man that thou dost care for him?" (8:3-4). Being out in nature can remind us of the awesome world in which we live and of God's care for us.

But as for me, I'll see you at the Holiday Inn Express where I will be watching the Nature Channel.

For Reflection and Discussion

• Do you take time to see the handiwork of God in nature? And if so, does it draw you closer to Him?
• What are our responsibilities as Christians to care for nature and respect God's creation?

Scripture: "And God saw all that He had made, and behold, it was very good" (Gen. 1:31).

Prayer: "Almighty God, I can see your work in nature and I thank you for the beauty of it and the inspiration that comes from it. Help me to take time to get close to the earth and away from the hectic life that I lead. Amen."

What's in a Name?

I love sports. I love to play them or watch them. At this point in my life I am doing more watching than playing, and I am not happy about that. Nonetheless, to fill the void in my sports addictions, I still have ESPN. How did I make it in life before the advent of ESPN? What was life like before that? I can't remember and can't fathom how miserable it must have been. What did I do before there was a SportsCenter and the "Top Ten Plays of the Week"? Sheri says that our home is a shrine to ESPN. The fact that the family portrait has been replaced by a life-size poster of Chris Berman could be a clue.

We love sports. Natalie has a basketball goal in the den along with two golf clubs. I hope that her hockey mask will be here by Christmas. Anyway, back in '04, ESPN celebrated its twenty-fifth anniversary with a special on their history. One of the interesting aspects of the program was to learn that some people across our great

---

What does your name mean?   Or better yet, are you living up to the name Christian?

---

land have named their new babies Espn. Or if it is a girl, they add a y, as in Espyn. Now why didn't I think of that for our daughter Natalie? Sheri and I had the hardest time coming up with a name, and it was right there on the TV screen every night.

Biblical names had meanings, but with a much deeper significance than sports. People in those days knew what their names meant and it was important to them.

The prophet Isaiah named his son Maher-shalal-hash-baz (Smith). (What was Isaiah thinking when he gave the poor boy that moniker?) The name means "the spoil speeds, the prey hastes," indicating that the enemy, Assyria, would invade Israel, which would be bad news.

What does your name mean? Or better yet, are you living up to the name Christian? There was a time when carrying the name Christian really meant something.

For Reflection and Discussion

• Does being a Christian really mean something to you or are you a Christian in name only?
• What qualities did Jesus have that you would like to emulate?

Scripture: "...and the disciples were first called Christians at Antioch" (Acts 11:26).

Prayer: "Father, I would like to live up to the name Christian, but I know how difficult it is to do. I sometimes fail to take my faith seriously, and I feel like a hypocrite when I profess one thing and do another. Forgive me. Amen."

"In this Corner..."

His cumulative record was 53-9-4 over a 27-year career, including victories over Floyd Patterson and Earnie Shavers. He was a surprisingly fast, hard hitter. He died in '99. Who was he? A boxer. Jerry Quarry. Remember him? Most will remember him as a punching bag for Muhammad Ali and Joe Frazier.

He had been hospitalized for pneumonia and had gone into cardiac arrest not long before his death. But really, neither of these were the real killers. He had spent the last years of his life with an illness called *dementia pugilistica*. In laymen's terms he was "punch drunk,"

What they don't need is for someone to kick them while they are down.

---

meaning his brain had died prematurely as a result of taking so many blows during his boxing career. In the last years of his life, he was unable to live alone and had to be shaved and fed by his mother and brother.

A neurologist, Dr. Ira Casson, urged Quarry not to continue fighting after a 1983 CAT scan. Yet he fought three more times, including a '92 comeback bout, in which he was pounded for a measly purse of $1,050.00. Casson says that Quarry is "living proof of what too many fights can do." He added: "The damage is cumulative."

How many Jerry Quarrys do you know? I'm not talking boxers. I mean people, friends and loved ones, who have taken blow after blow from life. Abuse. (Bang!)

Illness. (Pow!) Tragedy. (Zap!) And where do we find them? On the ropes. Going down for the count. Bruised and battered.

What they don't need is for someone to kick them while they are down. What they need is a trainer in their corner, someone to bandage their wounds and nurture them back to health. Then, after that, perhaps we can tell them about the one who was "wounded for our transgressions" and "by His bruises we are healed" (Isaiah 53:5).

I'm glad He fought in my place, aren't you?

For Reflection and Discussion

• Do you know people who have been "roughed up" by life, and if so, what are you doing to help them?
• How can you best help them, with words or with deeds?

Scripture: "Bear one another's burdens, and thus fulfill the law of Christ" (Galatians 6:2).

Prayer: "Lord, I sometimes get caught up in my own world and don't notice those around me who are hurting. Give me compassion for others that I might help in whatever meager way I can to alleviate their suffering. Amen."

Holy Hockey

The "Great One" retired back in '99. In case you don't know hockey lingo, I'm talking about Wayne Gretzky, who carried the moniker, "The Great One." Considered the greatest hockey player in the history of the sport, #99 called it quits in '99. He retired with lots of records: 10 scoring titles, nine MVPs, two play-off MVPs and four Stanley Cup rings.

I don't know much about hockey. Never played it. Growing up in south Alabama, we saw snow once a decade and never ice-skated. The only skating we did was roller-skating. In fact, I've only ice-skated once and

---

Because of the Incarnation, I believe God fully understands where we are in life.

---

it wasn't a pleasant experience. I spent more time trying to get up off the ice than I spent skating on it. After that disaster, I do really appreciate the power and skill of hockey players.

Hockey is too violent for my tastes. You've heard the old line: "I went to a boxing match and a hockey game broke out." I would like the sport better if it had less fighting.

I don't even know the rules of hockey. All I know is that when the puck goes into the net, it counts one point. That doesn't happen often since most hockey games are rather low scoring. I also know that a "hat trick" is when one player scores three goals in one game.

Take a Knee

It's hard to appreciate a sport or any other life experience, unless you've done it. For example, you can't really know what it is like to have and raise kids until you have had and raised kids. You can't fully understand the pain of grief until you have experienced the pain of grief. I can't fully understand another person's story unless I've walked in their shoes.

I believe God fully understands where we are in life. Because of the Incarnation, when God put on human flesh, He has (1) walked in our shoes (skates), (2) known our joy, and (3) felt our pain. Sounds like a "hat trick" to me.

For Reflection and Discussion

• How can I at least sympathize with others on my team even though I have not experienced the pain they are going through?
• Does God really understand all that I am going through?

Scripture: "And the Word became flesh, and dwelt among us…" (John 1:14).

Prayer: "Lord, I do believe that because you walked this earth, you do understand my joys and my pains. May I talk to you honestly about them and talk to others who struggle in life. Give me a tender and compassionate heart for others. Amen."

Perfection

Bowling is not my favorite sport. It ranks way down on my list, somewhere between horseshoes and tiddlywinks. I bowl about once a decade, or if dragged to a Sunday school bowling party, twice a decade. When I do bowl, I just try to keep it (the ball) between the gutters. (This, by the way, is not a bad philosophy of life.)

After reading an article by Rick Reilly in *Sports Illustrated*, I may have to go more often. He says the

---

Why is it so tough these days to have a strong family?

---

sport is getting easier. No, the pins aren't any lighter or the lanes wider. It's oil. Owners of bowling alleys are putting oil on the lanes so the ball will stay on the line where it is bowled. It's like a golfer putting in his bathtub. And the bowling balls are now built like a ton of bricks.

So with these hard-core, nuked bowling balls and oil slicked lanes, my dog D.D. could bowl a good score. In one recent year, 34,479 perfect games were rolled. A 10-year-old boy bowled 300. An 87-year-old man did as well. Dick Weber, one of the all-time greats, only had 14 perfect games in his career. There's a guy in Saginaw, Michigan, who has 59. Some guy in California has a 300 right-handed and left-handed. Gee whiz, what has the world come to? Why not give each bowler a ball and a bazooka? If you can't bowl 'em down, shoot 'em down.

Perfection ain't what it used to be. Life and sports shouldn't be that easy. Most of us in today's America have it too easy in bowling and life. There is too much wealth, too much food, too many conveniences, and too much entertainment.

Don't get me wrong. Some things are still tough – like relationships. Marriage is tough too, sometimes. Raising kids is fun but often difficult. Precisely because some things come so easy to us, (like wealth, food, conveniences and entertainment), maintaining a family often does not. We find it difficult, in part, because the pace and prosperity of modern life make relationships difficult. Heck, maintaining a strong family is as tough as bowling used to be!

For Reflection and Discussion

• Why is it so tough these days to have a strong family? Is it the pace of life or do too many other things, like sports, compete for our attention?
• Why do we find it so difficult to build a strong relationship with our spouse and kids? Does being involved with sports help or hurt?

Scripture: "Therefore encourage one another, and build up one another…" (1 Thessalonians 5:11).

Prayer: "Father, it is not easy to have a strong relationship with others, whether they are our parents, kids, teammates or a friend. We are tempted to spend too much time doing other things and not enough time encouraging those we love. Help us to work harder at these important relationships. Amen."

"Spare" Me

Talking about a bad night. The movie we wanted to see was sold out, and so Sheri and I gave in to our son, Tyler's, pleas. BOWLING. The game hasn't changed since I last bowled except that now a computer automatically keeps your score. I consider this a technological wonder because keeping score in bowling is like figuring out a Rubik's Cube. The computer also keeps the scorekeeper from cheating, which heretofore, had been my best bowling attribute.

So, Sheri, Tyler, and I put on those funny looking shoes, and I proceeded to teach them a thing or two about the sporting world. Well, a funny thing happened on the way to my acceptance speech. My lovely wife

---

From time to time, we all need to be taken to the woodshed (or bowling alley).

---

proceeded to bowl a 174 and whip my Baptist backside. One hundred and seventy four! She had seven strikes. I bowled a...well, it was considerably less than hers. I used every excuse imaginable (arthritic hip, aching back) because I hate to lose. She let me have it all the way home. "Have a little humble pie, dear – one hundred and seventy-four slices." To which I retorted, "Meet me on the golf course, a real man's game."

Most ministers I know need a small dose of humility. Some insist on being called "Doctor," when if fact, they haven't earned one. Others of us who have earned one can be equally arrogant, flaunting our titles. A ministerial calling leads some to think that they have all the answers and live on a different spiritual plane than common folk. Egos become enlarged when someone (a preacher) stands up before a crowd on Sunday morning with a big Bible and matching tie and hankie. From time to time, we all need to be taken to the woodshed (or bowling alley).

For Reflection and Discussion

• Does your ego ever become inflated when you do something good in sports? Is that a good or bad thing?
• Where is the line between being proud of your accomplishments and being arrogant about your ability?
• Is humility a good trait?

Scripture: "Blessed are the humble, for they shall inherit the earth" (Matthew 5:5).

Prayer: "Lord, I am proud of what I accomplish as an athlete and coach and yet I know I should always give credit to you and to all who have helped make me successful. Give me a dose of humility concerning the talents that I have. Amen."

"Drivers, Start your Engines"

So, what do NASCAR and speed skating on ice have in common? Read on. I've never been to a NASCAR event. Never. I drove past Talladega one time when all the motor homes were parked outside prior to the 500 – dropped my jaw at that sight.

I had dinner at an Italian restaurant across the street from the Daytona Speedway one time. Dropped the same jaw and uttered "golly gee" at the size of the place. But I have never been on the inside to actually watch a race.

Speed skating? Where would I go to watch it? I've roller-skated and raced other skaters around the rink.

I've seen some disciples of Jesus start out really fast but crash before the checkered flag.

Not a good idea. I know how it feels to fall on your backside while roller-skating, but ice-skating is like, from another planet or something.

So, why did I ask the question, what do they have in common, NASCAR and speed skating? Because I saw two remarkable events recently that brought them together. First, the Daytona 500. The guy who won it did so because all the racers in front had a big pile-up late in the race. All of a sudden he is in the lead with four or five laps to go, and all he has to do is keep the car on track and he wins. Same thing happened in Olympic Speed Skating. Five racers. Four crashed on the final turn and this one dude, who was in last and headed for a tin medal, skated home for the gold instead. Now, what do you think about that?

The "Tortoise and the Hare" fable comes to mind. The fastest don't always cross the finish line first. Same way in faith. I've seen some disciples of Jesus start out really fast but crash before the checkered flag. Likewise, I've seen disciples plod along, day by day. Inch here. Inch there. But they get the gold.

The race is on. I'll take a plodder any day.

For Reflection and Discussion

• Do you have a disciplined, metered faith that is steady in its day-to-day application to real life?
• Do you know Christians who started out with a bang, but faltered shortly after making their Christian profession?

Scripture: "…and let us run with perseverance the race that is set before us" (Hebrews 12:1).

Prayer: "Lord, teach me consistency and discipline in my faith and daily walk. Grant that I may walk with you faithfully every day and grow in my faith with each passing moment. Amen."

Run for the Roses

I kept waiting for him to say it, but he never did. It's a rite of spring. He always says it, and so I waited. He never said it. I promise. He has a small window of opportunity to say it and once that window is closed, it's too late. The "stretch" only lasts for a few seconds and if the announcer is going to say, "And down the stretch they come," then he had better come out with it. He didn't.

The Kentucky Derby is "the greatest two minutes in sports" (unless of course, you have watched me run a 100-meter-dash), and I look forward to it like an ice cream social. By the way, the greatest two minutes in sports became for me the greatest minute-and-a-half because as the race began, our daughter Natalie decided

---

Have you told your kids how much you love them? Say it while you can. The "stretch" doesn't last forever.

---

to grab the remote and turn off the TV. I screamed. But I got it on in time to see "the stretch."

And I promise he didn't say it. That's like not saying, "Drivers start your engines" at the Indy 500 or not singing, "Take Me Out to the Ballgame" at the seventh-inning stretch. Heck, it's like coming to church and not singing the Doxology. I love traditions. Oh, I know that sometimes traditions at church can become so set in stone that we never make any changes, and I know that is not good. But some traditions become places where we put down roots and reach deep into the history of the church. Rituals can be foundations for our lives that keep us grounded. I like them and that's why I was mad that the announcer didn't say, "And down the stretch they come."

We have a tradition at our home that we all like. When Tyler was an only child, we started the ritual of having a "Tyler sandwich" before he went to bed. Such a sandwich involved a hug from mom and dad (the bread) to Tyler (the meat). Since Natalie's arrival we have included her in the evening ritual, with her as the cheese. She loves it as we all share good night hugs and kisses.

Have you told your kids how much you love them? Say it while you can. The "stretch" doesn't last forever.

For Reflection and Discussion

• What family rituals do you have and why do you like or dislike them?
• How often do you tell your loved ones that you love them? Is it hard to do and if so, why?
• Are there team rituals that have meaning for you and why?

Scripture: "And now faith, hope, and love abide, these three; and the greatest of these is love" (1 Corinthians 13:13).

Prayer: "Father, thank you for the rituals in my family that remind me of our love for one another. Give me courage to tell those I love how much I care about them. Amen."

"Dad Gum"

I watched the Super Bowl and didn't utter one "dad gum" or "dag nab it" or "good grannies alive." I didn't curse either; in fact, I didn't come close. Of course I had no horse in the race or dog in the fight, i.e., I didn't really care who won. Now had I cared passionately for either team, I might have let something loose, like "dad blast it."

I watch a lot of sports, including high school games, and I can tell you how seriously people take their sports teams. Fans taunt other fans, players and even cheerleaders. About the most inflammatory cheer we had in high school was, "Beat 'um, bust 'um, that's our custom."

Well, hooray for Boston University, who this year ('07) has a rule that anybody who cusses at a BU home sporting event gets kicked out of the arena. Also, a

---

I have an even better suggestion; talk to one another like the Lord is listening. He is.

"thumbs up" to James V. O'Conner, author of *Cuss Control*, and director (I'm not making this up) of the Cuss Control Academy, who says we should use words that sound like cusses but aren't. So, you can yell at the referee, "That was Bolshevik," or shout to the rafters, "You son of a biscuit!" If these don't work, then O'Conner suggests we pretend that our grandma is listening.

I have an even better suggestion; talk to one another like the Lord is listening. He is. And He cares what we say to one another and to our enemies/opponents. Taunting others is never appropriate for Christians, and hate-filled language should not come out of our mouths. Jesus said, "Do not swear at all...but let your yes be yes" (Matthew 5:33-37). In other words, keep your !@#$&% to yourself and let your "dad gums be dad gums."

For Reflection and Discussion

• Why is it that in a heated moment of a sports event, we say things we shouldn't?
• When in a competitive game, how can I make sure that my language is appropriate?
• Where do we draw the line between good-natured ribbing and taunting?

Scripture: "But set the believers an example in speech and conduct" (1 Timothy 4:12).

Prayer: "Almighty God, sometimes the words that come from my mouth don't honor you or set a good example. Especially in the heat of competition, I occasionally lose my temper and say words that are inappropriate. Forgive me and help me. Amen."

Derby Dad

Once I took our then 3-year-old daughter, Natalie, to our community's annual May Fest celebration. A pony ride was available, and so we waited in line with, oh, about one million other youngsters. It was a safe experience, though one young boy screamed bloody murder, as if he had seen a girl in curlers for the first time. I mean it could not have been any safer for the kids, as the four ponies were strapped to a pole and harnessed, walking in a very small circle, with the children on top, yelling "giddy up." I like safe stuff, especially when the kids are involved.

I couldn't help but contrast that with what would happen later that afternoon, with the "Run for the Roses," at The Kentucky Derby. Horse racing at Churchill Downs ain't

---

How far should we go as parents and coaches to protect our children?

---

safe. Those fast and powerful horses run at break-neck speeds, spurred on by daring jockeys, around a much bigger circle. I felt safe and comfortable watching Natalie ride the ponies, but how would I feel if it were my daughter or son riding one of those mounts in The Derby?

The truth is, we want our children to be safe, and if we had our way, they would pick vocations that are safe. And yet, in the same breath, we encourage them to follow the Lord's leading. One of the favorite hymns in our church is "Wherever He Leads I'll Go," but do we really mean those words and do we want our children to go "wherever," if it means Africa or the Middle East? I have a friend who has two daughters, one who has been recently in Afghanistan as a missionary, and another daughter who wants to go to Africa and help the poor. He asked them where they got that calling. They said, "We got it from you dad. You told us to follow the Lord." He said to his daughters, "I was kidding." But he wasn't. And they knew it. If we can get our kids to (1) use their talents for the Lord, (2) surrender to His will, and (3) give Him the glory, then we are talking about some kind of special Triple Crown.

For Reflection and Discussion

• Sports involve some risk, especially the risk of injury. How do you deal with that fear?
• How far should we go as parents and coaches to protect our children?

Scripture: "My father, if it is possible, let this cup pass from me; yet not as I will, but as Thou wilt" (Matthew 26:39).

Prayer: "Father, we sing the hymn, 'Wherever He Leads I'll Go,' but I don't always mean it. I am afraid of what the future holds and afraid to let go of my life and my children's lives. Help me to trust you for the present and the future. Amen."

Concession Stand

I've spent a good portion of my life at concession stands. Why? For one, I love to eat and two, I love ball games. And so I have eaten my fair share of hot dogs and hamburgers at concession stands. Sheri and I have, in fact, celebrated our wedding anniversary with a concession stand hot dog. I've stood in many a line on a Friday night waiting impatiently for someone to get my order, take my money and bring me my food, so I wouldn't miss much of the game.

Now, all that has changed. Oh, I'm still going to frequent concession stands, but it will be from a different perspective. It has all changed because one Friday night, I worked the concession stand at a football game. Or should I say, it worked me. From the time we

---

Why is it so easy to judge others before we have "walked in their shoes"?

---

arrived at about 5:30, until we had cleaned up after the game at about 10:30, we went non-stop. Did I see any of the game? No. Did I see any of the wonderful half-time show? No. Did I have time to eat supper? No. We worked.

I looked up the word "concession" in the dictionary. It can mean a business or it can mean conceding something, as in "surrender." The latter definition is the one that fit that Friday evening. About half-time, I was ready to concede or surrender. The little white flag dangling from the money register was from "yours truly."

So, the next time I stand in line waiting for service and food, and someone behind the counter is scrambling to get the order and change right, I will have a different attitude. I might stop and say a prayer for them or at least, offer a word of thanks for their service. And the next time you walk into worship, know that behind the scenes, the choir and secretarial/ministerial staff have been working hard to make it all happen. And, Lord only knows, how hard your coaches work before and after practice to put the best possible team on the field. Thank them too.

For Reflection and Discussion

• Why is it easy to judge others before we have "walked in their shoes"?
• How can we be more sympathetic to those who work so hard behind the scenes at church or at a ballgame and be more grateful for their work?

Scripture: "For in the same way you judge, you will be judged" (Matthew 7:2).

Prayer: "Almighty God, I tend to lose patience with others when, in truth, I don't know how hard their lives and work are. Help me to be more sympathetic with others and more appreciative of those who work so hard to make my life what it is. Amen."

Clichés

The sports world is loaded with clichés, such as "I gave 110%" (which, by the way, is impossible to do), "take it one game at a time" (how else could you take it?) and "it ain't over till it's over" (brought to you by the Department of Redundancy Department). Well, there is a new cliché, and we might as well get used to it and make the most of it. It is a five-word line: "It is what it is."

Do you want proof that this phrase is now the most over-used cliché in the wide world of sports? I'll give you proof. What did Bill Belichick, coach of the New England Patriots say after his assistant coach, Charlie Weiss, left for the job at Notre Dame? "It is what it is. We'll deal with it." Want more? Jeff Gordon, NASCAR driver, on an exchange of words with a cameraman, said, "Somebody sort of egged me on, and it is what it is. I can't take it back." Mike Minter, safety for the NFL's Carolina Panthers, on his team's start one season, "Never in a million years did I think we would be 1-5 at

---

We cannot let things that cannot be changed paralyze us.

---

this juncture, but it is what it is." Had enough? Apparently NASCAR driver Jimmy Johnson wants the title of cliché king. When asked about finishing second in the Nextel Cup Championship, he responded with two: "We showed up and gave 110%, and it is what it is." I've got more, but I will spare you because you are probably reaching the point of cliché nausea.

So, what does "It is what it is" mean? Psychologist Dan Powell says the phrase means, "It happened. I'm going to forget about it. I'm going to move on ... There is nothing that can be done about it."

Theologian Reinhold Niebuhr was probably (no duh) a much deeper thinker than the aforementioned sports stars, but his Serenity Prayer has much the same line of thinking: "Lord, grant me the serenity to accept the things I cannot change ..."

We cannot undo the past, and bad choices cannot be unmade. There are illnesses and diseases that are not going to be cured today or next month or next year. We cannot let the things that can't be changed paralyze us. We must accept some things and then move on with our lives. Hey, "It is what it is," and that's more than a cliché. It's the truth.

For Reflection and Discussion

• How do you accept things that you cannot control on the sports field, such as bad calls and bad bounces?
• Are you able to forget the bad things that happen and move on to what lies ahead?

Scripture: "...but this one thing I do: forgetting what lies behind and straining forward to what lies ahead" (Philippians 3:13).

Prayer: "Lord, help me to accept those things that happen in sports and in life that are beyond my control. And give me the strength to forget the past and concentrate my energy on what is ahead of me. Amen."

"Kick it"

It's not that I hate soccer, because I don't. In fact, the only sport that I hate is synchronized swimming, which I only have to watch every four years at the Olympics, and even then, I quickly turn to an AFLAC commercial for relief. Natalie has signed up to play "you know what," and we are excited to watch her play. I've never understood or appreciated a sport where you can't use your hands, but there must be something great that the rest of the world sees. Soccer is huge world-wide, but not in the Davis household, at least not yet. We're getting there slowly. Nonetheless, Natalie is on the White-Hats team and her coach is named Alex. He works at a prison, by the way, a vocation which might come in handy when trying to coach 4-year olds which direction to run.

Anyway, the instructional letter from the Recreation Department to the parents emphasized that we are playing for fun and no score will be kept. Yeah right. The score will be kept in my head and in all the kids' heads. On the morning of Natalie's first practice, her first words, before "Good morning dad," were "Do you think my team will win some games?" I wonder where

---

I know that unbridled competition leads to conflict.

---

she got that competitive spirit. I mean, just because we have temporarily suspended the reading of children's books at night, and replaced them with Pele's life story, so what's the big deal about that? And just because we have her kicking soccer balls at 6:30 every morning and watching World Cup replays at night, why would you think that I am competitive?

The Recreation Department also told the parents not to yell "kick it" to the kids during the game. I've signed up for some language classes to learn how to say "kick it" in Spanish, French and Russian. Don't get me wrong. The Rec. Department has it right and they should discourage parents from getting too involved and they should stress that winning isn't everything. The problem is not with the Rec. Department, the problem is with me.

I know. I know. I know. Jesus said that the "first shall be last and the last shall be first" in the Kingdom of God (Mark 10:31). I know that unbridled competition leads to conflict. I also know that our worth shouldn't be measured against the performance of others. I know. But, how do you say "kick it" in Russian?

For Reflection and Discussion

• How can we stress the joy of the game when there is so much emphasis on winning?
• When is our striving to win too much and when does it become destructive?

Scripture: "Do nothing from selfish ambition or conceit, but in humility regard others as better than yourselves" (Philippians 2:3-4).

Prayer: "Lord, grant me humility that I may wish the best for my opponents and give you the praise when things do go my way. Amen."

Index

Take a Knee

**Humorous and Inspiring
Devotionals from
the World of Sports**

Steve Davis

For orders of ten or more, the book price is reduced to $10.00 per copy. For inquiries, Steve Davis may be reached at: steve@carrolltonfirstbaptist.com.

www.ingramcontent.com/pod-product-compliance
Lightning Source LLC
LaVergne TN
LVHW021350080426
835508LV00020B/2210